Two Suns
and a Green Sky

22 out-of-this-world weather models and experiments

Two Suns and a Green Sky

22 out-of-this-world weather models and experiments

Thomas Richard Baker

TAB Books

Division of McGraw-Hill, Inc.

New York   San Francisco   Washington, D.C.   Auckland   Bogotá
Caracas   Lisbon   London   Madrid   Mexico City   Milan
Montreal   New Delhi   San Juan   Singapore
Sydney   Tokyo   Toronto

FIRST EDITION
FIRST PRINTING
© 1994 by **Thomas Richard Baker**.
TAB Books is a division of McGraw-Hill, Inc.

Library of Congress Cataloging-in-Publication Data

ISBN 0051437-0

Editorial team: Kimberly Tabor, Acquisitions editor
       Jim Gallant, Editor
       David M. McCandless, Managing editor
       Joanne M. Slike, Executive editor
Production team: Katherine G. Brown, Director
       Patsy D. Harne, Desktop operator
       Nancy K. Mickley, Proofreading
       Marty Ehrlinger, Computer illustrator
Design team: Jaclyn J. Boone, Designer
       Brian Allison, Associate Designer

TAB1
0051437

Dedication

My daughter and I have shared a great many stories over the years, and one about a beautiful Magic Pony has become her favorite. Each story has imaginative weather occurrences as directed by Noel.

This second weather book arose from a condition that Noel placed on the clouds over the mythical Ponyland, a planet so far away even the weather has constraints placed on it.

These clouds are not permitted to make rain. I accept that restriction. If you try it with your children, you'll find it possesses a certain charm, especially for those younger than eight.

I dedicate this book to Noel Catherine Baker. Thank you, my beautiful girl, for just being you.

Thanks to TAB/McGraw-Hill in Blue Ridge Summit, Pennsylvania, for the wonderful assistance I have received from Kim Tabor, Steve Bolt, Sally Straight, Kim Martin, and all the others. You're terrific people.

Contents

APPENDICES

Foreword

This is the latest of Tom Baker's books that make our weather the object of experimentation and excitement to the space-age and "Star Trek" generation.

It challenges gifted students to open their minds to other-world weather, creative labs, and real scientific thought. The average student is caught up in these activities because of the ease and simplicity of each lesson.

Mr. Baker helps create success with fill in data charts and graphs. Not surprisingly, these labs can also be demonstrations for elementary classes where teachers are hard put for new methods to teach about weather.

Mr. Baker is a natural science teacher, but it was very low among his choices for a lifetime vocation. He served as an officer on the City of Burbank Police Department, as a radio engineer for a Los Angeles station, a technical writer for Northrop Corporation, and spent an entire spring as a working treasure hunter in the Caribbean.

Variety is a part of this good teacher's background. In 1986, he became a substitute teacher, found his life's work, and surrendered to the classroom.

His tenure was interrupted by Desert Storm, during which he served in the Persian Gulf as a petty officer radioman in the United States Coast Guard.

Mr. Baker's ability to create new lab experiences has been a blessing to coworkers and his students.

This book was written because there was a need. During his college education (California State University, Northridge), Baker's weather professor told the class, "there is a dearth of investigative laboratory classes based on weather."

At a National Science Teachers convention in Kansas City, teachers told him, "we can't teach weather labs because we don't have the facilities or materials." The challenge was there.

Baker spent time in his classroom lab before and after school doing and redoing unique experiments. The result was his very successful *Weather in the Lab*, which simulated natural phenomena.

It was the great (late) Dr. Isaac Asimov's pronouncement that "planets have a certain air about them" that started Baker thinking about this book.

Baker notes that each planet in our solar system is different and asks if the weather possibilities of other solar systems are just as different. He asks how pressure, temperature, and relative humidity vary in a carbon dioxide atmosphere. The student is then shown how to find out.

What are the book's strengths and weaknesses? There are not enough pages for all the possible experiments, such as a forecast with two suns (red giant and blue dwarf). Still, you can do this on your own along with all the other additional experiments suggested in the book's back pages.

A major strength of the book is that it does not call for special equipment. Baker's suggested sources for apparatus include garage sales.

His experiment setups are extremely visual and emulate larger models. He is a perfectionist and has done each of these labs many times before writing it down. The ability to predict consistent results, though they may vary in different classrooms around the country, is most satisfying to the lab teacher.

Over the years, I have watched and admired Baker's classroom exuberance excite usually bored students, as he received applause at NSTA conventions for his solid science, and as his barometer was featured in the Weather section of *USA Today*.

This book is fun, unique, and has an unusual approach.

Dr. George R. Fischbeck
Eyewitness News Weather Service
KABC-TV
Los Angeles, California

Preface

Making the experiment setup is an experiment in itself. You and your students will enjoy planting seeds in preparation for an ultraviolet "sunshine," making a carbon dioxide atmosphere from exhausting the oxygen in a sealed chamber, and preparing a "red giant" and "blue dwarf" binary sun system prior to heating the surface of a hypothetical planet.

While a purist may object and claim this is not a "weather" book, look closely. It is a weather book with more disciplines added. Biology, oceanography, physical science, atmospherics, and hydrology are just a few that are explored. Once again, the study of weather and climate demonstrates how tightly interwoven they are within the other scientific disciplines.

These are the speculative experiments, the "what if" approaches to classroom learning that must be used with our students. These exercises go beyond our Earth and speculate on the types of weather on other planets.

It has been said that imagination is more important than knowledge. This is quite true. However, wonder is more important than imagination. A question raised about an occurrence in our natural world leads to an exploration of the phenomenon and eventually to knowledge based on experimentation.

This experimentation occurs with models. It is not easy to define "good" model. Ideally, it should correctly predict the results and raise a new question from the exercise performed. Your models will differ from mine. Your results will be somewhat different also. The key to performing well is to make all models consistent with one another. If a lamp is 25 cm away from a substance being heated, be sure that it is the same distance in the next experiment as well.

Visualize physical phenomena here on this planet. Certain physical laws govern these events. The possibilities of these phenomena could very likely occur on some other planet.

Please keep in mind these are open-ended exercises. My results are merely guides. I obtained consistency during a summer month within certain temperatures, pressures and humidity levels in my lab at Thousand Oaks High School. There are some things I can't completely explain.

Enjoy!

Introduction

In this second book, I've stressed the data gathering and analyses in each laboratory exercise.

These experiments were written for the middle and high school level student. They can be performed (as a demonstration) quite successfully for students from the kindergarten level to the sixth grade.

Grade school students are innately curious. Data access and analysis need not be stressed with the younger students. Often, the functioning model will help these budding scientists to visualize the outside "real life" occurrence.

These laboratory experiments are also explorations. They cannot be absolutes. It would be difficult to say with a high degree of certainty how the atmosphere on Venus, for example, maintains its high temperatures.

Lastly, these exercises must be used as springboards to delve further into a concept being discussed in the science book used.

I have generated a few standards to help you in interpreting the data from my exercises.

First, a 100-watt lamp (white) 25 cm above a pan or test tube containing substances being heated approximates a sunny Southern California day at local noon in July. That was my standard for indoor experiments.

Second, an "atmosphere" used refers to an aquarium sealed off from outside influencing factors. During the preparation of a carbon dioxide "atmosphere" in an aquarium, some water vapor is generated. There are some smoke particles as well. Obviously, the nitrogen remains in the tank, but there is enough carbon dioxide to obtain satisfactory results from the exercise being performed.

I wanted ease in preparation of any exercise, coupled with the accessibility of any equipment, to be of paramount importance. Inexpensive, good quality equipment will provide fairly accurate and consistent results.

If any of you scientific readers and experimenters establish easier methods for conducting these labs (or develop new ideas), please write them down. If anyone in the science world would take time to send their suggestions, observations, and comments, I would greatly appreciate them. Only in this way can future texts be sharpened.

Thank you.

Thomas Richard Baker
c/o TAB Books
13311 Monterey Lane
Blue Ridge Summit, PA 17294

Lab safety procedures

1. Wear goggles or safety glasses when any type of heating occurs. It is good safety procedure to wear goggles at all times during any science experiment.
2. When preparing glass tubing or thermometers for insertion over rubber stoppers, use glycerin or liquid soap and water.
3. Avoid looking at the sun or light from any lamp. This includes the 100-watt red, green, blue, and white lamps. In particular, avoid looking at the 75-watt ultraviolet lamp.
4. Observe all manufacturer safety precautions in the handling of all chemicals—liquid, solid, or gaseous. Wash hands thoroughly after leaving the laboratory. Wash hands immediately if any chemical touches the skin. Consult a lab safety manual for the safe handling of any chemicals if manufacturer's safety precautions are not available.
5. Observe all safety precautions with heating devices and lamps, and handle all heated materials with care.
6. Be sure electrical cords are coiled away from any sink or pans filled with water.
7. Use masking tape strips to tape thermometers to the glass walls of an aquarium.
8. Wear goggles when making a smoke source, such as burning newspaper.
9. Wear gloves or use towels when handling any glass panes that have been cut. Tape these edges with fiberglass-lined tape to reduce any chance of injury.
10. Clean all spills of water with towels or a mop.
11. Use a broom and dustpan to pick up any broken pieces of glassware. Dispose of any broken items in appropriate containers.
12. Dispose of solid waste in appropriate containers, not in the sink.
13. During periods of violent weather, all weather forecasts and observations must

be made with extreme caution and personal safety in mind.

14. Report all accidents, spills, and injuries in the laboratory (no matter how small) to your instructor at once.

15. Avoid contact with any chemical—solid, liquid, or gas.

16. When preparing the alcohol thermometer that is used in the appendix labelled "Fun Phenomena," be extremely careful in pushing the rubber stopper and glass tubing into the Erlenmeyer flask opening.

17. Completely follow all directions given by your instructor.

18. Perform any experiment, whether in the lab at school or at home, under constant supervision by an adult (your instructor or parents).

19. Wear goggles when using the vacuum/blower nozzle during the experiment that uses sand particles.

About the safety icons

Throughout this book, you will find special safety icons. These icons mean the following:

 Students need adult supervision for this activity.

 Be careful of the heat generated by the lamp(s).

 Do not stare at the lamp(s). Eye damage could result.

 For safety, you need special equipment such as gloves or goggles.

 Be careful to avoid burns and/or cuts.

Experiment preparation techniques

LAB SIZE AND LENGTH

The following lab lengths (periods or hours) and size of group (maximum four students, unless it is a demonstration) are to be used as a guide in determining the amount of teaching time apportioned to each experiment.

Experiment #	Length (periods/hours)	Group size
1	2	4
2	2	4
3	2	4
4	2	4
5	1	class
6	2	4
7	2	4
8	2	4
9	2	4
10	2	4
11	2-4	class
12	1	4
13	2-4	class
14	2	4
15	2-4	class
16	1-2	class
17	1-2	4
18	1-2	4
19	1-2	class
20	1-2	class
21	2-3	class

GRAPHING HINTS

1. Always use a straightedge that is longer than the paper you are using.
2. Always use a number two pencil.
3. Use graph paper that is four squares to the inch.
4. Make the coordinate axes for both the Y and the X five boxes in and five boxes up on the graph sheet.
5. Orient the graph sheet for maximum readability: "landscape" means the X axis is the longer side; "portrait" means the Y axis is the longer side.
6. Choose an appropriate scale to completely fit the data you have recorded.
7. For multiple lines, use a set of colored pencils.
8. Label all X and Y axes with the appropriate titles and units used.
9. Be sure to title the graph you have made, preferably in black ink.
10. Don't write anything on the reverse side of the graph sheet—this ensures readability by your lab partners and instructor.
11. The lines on a sheet of graph paper can be used for any scale. However, don't subdivide more closely than one-half of a box.
12. *Time,* as measured in minutes or seconds, is an independent variable. Be sure to place it on the X axis. Use the appropriate scale to fit the time interval recorded.
13. *Temperature,* as measured in degrees Celsius, is a dependent variable. Place it on the Y axis. Use a scale that includes the lowest to the highest temperatures.

PREPARATION TECHNIQUES

Carbon dioxide/nitrogen atmosphere

For Experiments, 12, 14, 15, 16, and 17, wear goggles when handling the glass or using any open flames.

An aquarium that does not leak water must be used. Obtain a glass cover (cut to size from a local hardware store) that makes a snug fit with the rim. Tape fiberglass tape (¼ inch) around the sharp edges. This will help protect against cuts. Use gloves when handling any cut glass.

I used a "tea" candle to consume the oxygen in my aquarium. Since it generates enough heat to crack the top cover, I placed six heating screens over this candle. Any less, and the top would crack. (This knowledge is empirically based from personal experience.)

After the candle flame goes out, the amount of oxygen is appreciably less than the approximately 20% normally found in air. The heat from the flame affects the temperature within the tank only slightly.

During the making of this carbon dioxide gas, the aquarium walls will have water vapor condense on them. After the candle flame goes out, wait at least 10 minutes before beginning any experiment that calls for this prepared "atmosphere."

However, there are experiments that simply cannot wait for this water vapor to condense. The procedures in such experiments will supersede these directions. Your results should not be greatly affected by this vapor.

Different salinity "oceans"

For Experiments 15 and 18, use the following formulae. The percentage by mass of a solution equals (mass of solute)/(mass of solute + mass of solvent):

3.5% NaCl = 3.5 g of NaCl/(3.5 g NaCl + 96.5 ml of distilled water)
7.0% NaCl = 7.0 g of NaCl/(7.0 g NaCl + 93 ml of distilled water)
10.0% NaCl= 10.0 g of NaCl/(10.0 g NaCl + 90 ml of distilled water)

Note: Because the density of distilled water is close to 1.0 g/ml, the above volumes of water are equal masses.

These preparations will provide the correct percentage of each solution. (These amounts are only for 100 ml of the solution.) If a greater amount is needed, multiply the above amounts accordingly.

For Experiments 2, 3, 4, 6, 7, 13, 14, and 22, use samples of sand, dirt, grass, salt water, and tap water in test tubes (or other appropriate containers) with alcohol thermometers. Be sure the sand and dirt samples are dry and do not have rocks in them.

Prepare the salt solution (3.5% NaCl) using the preparation techniques in the preceding text.

Be sure to obtain only grass blades, not the dirt-covered roots.

Sand refers to beach sand or sand used in a child's sandbox.

Use only a one-hole rubber stopper and glycerin or soapy water, to twist the stopper onto the thermometer.

Push the stopper/thermometer assembly into the mouth of a clean and dry test tube. The rubber stopper should be firmly seated into the test tube.

Be sure the thermometer bulb extends into the substance (in the test tube) by at least 2 centimeters.

Simulation of a "noon day" sun

100 watt white lamp placed 25 cm above the object(s) being heated approximately equals a (local) noon hour sunny, summer (windless) day in Southern California. This standard was used for the indoor experiments when it was required.

Any heating temperatures obtained this way approximately equal (in terms of the slope of the lines drawn) any object actually heating in the outside sunlight.

Cutting glass tubing

When cutting glass tubing, use the following steps:

1. Wear goggles
2. Wear heavy gloves
3. Use adult supervision when needed
4. Do not cut glass tubing into pieces shorter than 15 cm (6 inches)

Using a metal triangular file, cut a notch in the glass for the desired length. *Do not cut* any additional notches! The glass could break unevenly!

Wrap the glass tubing in a paper towel.

Break the tubing at the notch.

Discard any broken pieces of glass in the appropriate containers.

Throw the paper towel away.

Fire polishing of glass tubing

When fire polishing glass tubing use the following steps:

1. Wear goggles
2. Wear heavy gloves
3. Use adult supervision when needed
4. Do not fire polish glass pieces shorter than 15 cm (6 inches)

Use a bunsen burner properly adjusted. At the bottom of the burner is a thumb screw. Turn this in either direction to regulate the amount of gas.

The long cylindrical neck of the burner can be twisted in either direction. This regulates the amount of oxygen to the flame.

When the burner is lit, a BLUE triangular flame indicates that the correct mixture of air and methane gas is being used. The flame will also have a small "roar" sound to it.

Place the cut end of the tubing into the tip of the blue flame (this is the hottest section). Twist the tubing constantly. A yellow portion of the flame will appear. This is due to the element sodium (used in the processing of the glass) burning off.

As the tubing edge heats, it will gain a rounded appearance. It will have a look of cooked candy.

Remove the glass tubing and place on a lab table (made of mineral rock). Be sure the tubing does not roll off the table. Let it cool for at least 10 minutes. CAUTION! Heated glass and cooled glass look exactly the same.

Methods that "failed"

I tried making a carbon dioxide atmosphere using a large pan of baking soda and vinegar. Since the gas generated is heavier than air, I thought it will displace the existing oxygen in the tank and leave me with a relatively pure source of carbon dioxide.

It didn't work. I ended up pouring too much vinegar into the pan. Of course, it bubbled and overflowed. It also produced a great deal of water vapor from the bubbling action. I will keep this method, however, because perhaps it can be used in another experiment.

Using the six heating screens stacked together does not imply a magic number. I arrived at this amount after burning my hand on the glass lid of the aquarium several times.

The lid of the tank was cracked twice. (Each lid costs approximately $3.00.) Finally, at six screens, the glass cover did not heat appreciably and did not crack.

Required equipment

The following equipment is required for the performance of the twenty-five laboratory experiments:

- aquarium: glass (a tank holding between 15–30 gallons works quite well)
- glass cover: cut to size to fit the above tank
- masking tape
- fiberglass tape (¼ inch)
- lamps: 100-watt red, green, blue, and white
- lamp: 75-watt ultraviolet
- lamp shield
- ring stand
- ring stand clamp
- alcohol thermometer
- globe of the Earth
- metal wire heating screen
- candle
- candle holder
- liquid crystal demonstration square—measures 6"×6" and is sensitive to the heat from a person's hand.
- goggles
- matches
- evaporating dish
- triple beam balance
- 10-ml graduated cylinder
- test tubes
- rubber stoppers (single hole) to fit the test tubes
- Erlenmeyer flask
- 500-ml beaker
- test tube rack

- methyl alcohol (burner fuel)
- isopropyl (rubbing) alcohol
- distilled water
- table salt or reagent grade NaCl (this won't make the water cloudy)
- clock or watch with second hand
- green transparency (the size of a normal sheet of notebook paper, 8.5"×11")

Garage sale tips

Should you purchase commercially? *Yes* and *no* are the answers. Some pieces of equipment, such as the liquid crystal panel, heating screen, and glassware must be purchased through a reputable equipment manufacturer.

Other equipment, such as the aquarium, tape, and glass panel can (and should) be purchased at my favorite "shopping malls" of all, the weekend garage sale.

Use common sense in buying any electrical items. These are often sold "as is" unless the person selling it is willing to take it back if it doesn't work.

I find that if I approach the sale from the standpoint that everything is a quarter to a dollar (to facilitate the sale), I can easily load my truck with five to ten dollars worth of good, used equipment. (I have the unfortunate affliction of being a pack rat!)

If what you've bought is in fairly good condition, it will give you years of good service. If it breaks, you are assured that its breakage does not mean an expensive loss.

Go out and go bargain hunting! You'll enjoy meeting new people and filling your lab with good "stuff."

The Sun

As a traveler to distant worlds beyond our own, you have certain strong notions about the Earth and her governing physical laws. These physical laws extend throughout the Universe. Your journey begins on Earth.

Your journey will be made through the experimenter's mind, because no manned space vehicles have gone beyond the Moon, though plenty of information has been sent to us from a number of satellites.

No one has yet discovered a planet orbiting a sun beyond our solar system. Such a discovery of a Jupiter-sized planet (or even one the Earth's size) would be a humbling experience.

As an astronaut on a voyage to this newly discovered planet what observations or data would you bring back to scientists?

Planets most certainly exist (I prefer to be optimistic). You would, however, first encounter the sun (or suns) of this planet.

On a clear night, away from the intrusive polluting lights of a nearby city, it is possible to see thousands of stars. These are suns of various sizes, ages, shapes and temperatures.

Sir Arthur S. Eddington, an English astronomer, proved that a star pulls its outer layers together with gravity. When the star shrinks, the core heats up. Heat then, makes the star expand. This "yoyo" effect, constant shrinking and contracting, occurs at temperatures in the millions of degrees at the core. The star becomes stable when contraction equals expansion.

A larger star has a higher core temperature, and therefore, generates more light.

The largest star ever observed is one with a mass 140 times that of our Sun. (It is listed in the Henry Draper Catalogue as HD 47129.) It is a binary system, however, each star having a mass 70 times our Sun's (both are the same size).

In some binary systems with stars of different sizes, the stars move around each other under a pull of gravity with a center of gravity between them. This center is always directly between them. The smaller star is farther away from it; the larger star is closer.

The orbit of such stars forms an ellipse. Inhabitants on a planet orbiting around such a binary system would see the two stars revolve about each other, one occasionally hiding the other's light.

The star's closest approach to this planet is called the periastron, Greek for "near the star," and the farthest position of this same star is the apastron, "away from the star."

How would such a planet heat and cool under the influence of these two stars? What would sunrises look like? Is there life on planets with binary stars?

The next few experiments explore the influence on a planet's possible weather by several different model suns.

1
The red giant (a convection cycle)

A red giant is a sun in the last stages of its life. Its outer layers of gas are red because they are cooler than the interior. Gaseous helium is fusing into carbon. Red giants are very large stars.

In 5 billion years, our sun will swell into such a star. Mercury, Venus, and Earth will become "comets," their atmospheres stripped away by the expansion of this red furnace.

Some of the outer planets could possibly be habitable by man or by other creatures. However, hypothesize with me for a moment. What would the heating temperatures on such a planet be like with a red giant for its sun?

Where would any life maintain shelter? Would vegetation be mobile to avoid intense "noon" temperatures? Would the pigmentation of this living matter be of the same color as the spectrum of light given off by this blazing swollen red giant?

This experiment is a simple model for producing a convection cycle, a "wind" on this hypothetical planet.

PURPOSE

The purpose of this experiment is to observe a simple convection cycle generated by a model of a "red sun."

MATERIALS NEEDED

- aquarium
- glass cover
- 500 ml beaker
- 100-watt red lamp
- 100-watt white lamp (if performed indoors)
- 2 lamp shields
- 1 ring stand with clamp
- masking tape
- 9 alcohol thermometers
- ice cubes
- clock or watch with second hand

PROCEDURE

1. See FIG. 1-1 for experiment set-up.
2. Tape the thermometers to the inside front wall of the tank. Be sure the readings are visible to the students recording data.
3. Fill a 500-ml beaker with five to seven ice cubes.
4. Attach a 100-watt red lamp to a lamp shield and fasten to the ring stand with the clamp.
5. Place the lamp over the top of the aquarium at the end opposite the beaker of ice cubes.
6. Record all beginning temperatures on FIG. 1-2.
7. Turn the lamp on.
8. Record temperatures every five minutes in FIG. 1-2.
9. At the end of 10 minutes, turn the lamp off.
10. Let it cool to room temperature before taking it apart.
11. See FIG. 1-3. for example recorded data (red lamp).
12. See FIG. 1-4. for example recorded data (performed in sunlight).

OBSERVATIONS

How quickly did the temperatures over the ice change from the beginning temperatures? Did they experience a downward trend?

How quickly did the "sun" temperatures change from the beginning temperatures?

QUESTIONS

Try this experiment with a blue bulb. Compare your readings to those obtained with the blue bulb. Which sun heats more intensely? (Remember these are merely colored lamps. Red light is cooler and blue light is warmer. Contrast this notion to a person painting the inside of a house with "warm red" or "cool blue.")

Did both suns reach the same temperatures?

EARTH EVENT

Use the 100-watt white lamp to repeat the experiment. How quickly did the temperatures change compared to the red lamp?

As an additional exercise, graph the example data from FIGS. 1-3. & 1-4. with your own data.

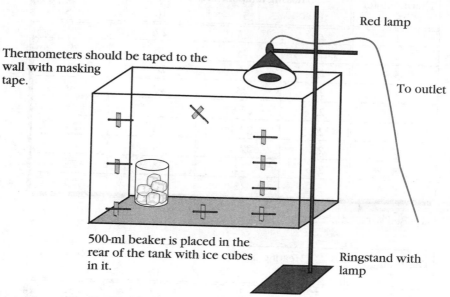

Standard glass-walled aquarium with glass cover

Red lamp

Thermometers should be taped to the wall with masking tape.

To outlet

500-ml beaker is placed in the rear of the tank with ice cubes in it.

Ringstand with lamp

1-1 Red giant experiment setup

Thermometer #	Heating temperatures every 5 minutes (°C)			
	0	5	10	15
1				
2				
3				
4				
5				
6				
7				
8				
9				

1-2 Red giant data table

Thermometer #	Heating temperatures every 5 minutes (°C)			
	0	5	10	15
1	22	23	27	28
2	22	23	28	29
3	22	23	28	30
4	22	23	28	30
5	22	22.5	25	25
6	22	22.5	24	24
7	22	22.5	24	24
8	22	22	23	23
9	22	22	25	25

I-3   Red giant sample data table (red lamp)

Thermometer #	Heating temperatures every 5 minutes (°C)			
	0	5	10	15
1	27	30	31	32
2	27	30	31	32
3	27	31	32	33
4	27	31	32	33
5	27	29	30	31
6	27	29	30	31
7	27	28	29	31
8	27	27	28	29
9	27	30	31	33

I-4   Red giant sample data table (outside sunlight)

☆ ☆ FACTOIDS ☆ ☆

The following facts have been paraphrased from a variety of sources (nearly 400): TV, magazines, research papers, newspapers, and reference books:

- Yeast can live in atmospheric pressure 8000 times Earth's sea level pressure (14.7 pounds psi).
- In the upper 63 miles of Earth's crust, the temperature increases 1° Fahrenheit every 150 feet down.

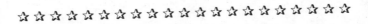

2
The ultraviolet sun (heating/cooling of actual land forms)

Let's assume a sun you've encountered is giving off some visible light, but high frequency visible blue and ultraviolet light. Your measurements show this light to be rich in ultraviolet rays.

Assuming there is an atmosphere on this planet, how would the heat from this sun affect the heating of the landscape? Is it possible that life would not exist on such a planet? Could such simple life be mobile enough to hide in rock outcroppings and survive at subsistence level?

In any case, the landscape will heat and cool at a certain rate. Most likely, the rates of heating and cooling will be quite different from the rates as observed from using our own sun.

PURPOSE

The purpose of this experiment is to observe the heating and cooling of actual samples of various land forms using an ultraviolet lamp as the heating "sun."

The data obtained here will be compared to that obtained in regular sunlight and a lamp simulating sunlight.

MATERIALS NEEDED

- test tube rack
- 5 test tubes
- 5 rubber stoppers (single hole)
- 5 alcohol thermometers
- 1 UV lamp—75 watts
- 1 75-watt white lamp
- 2 lamp shields
- 1 ring stand with clamp
- samples of: dry sand and dirt; grass blades (fresh), tap water, salt water (3.5% NaCl)
- clock or watch with second hand

PROCEDURE

1. See FIG. 2-1 for experiment setup.
   Be sure the ultraviolet lamp is at least 25 cm away from the substances being heated.
2. Record all beginning temperatures on FIG. 2-2.
3. Turn the lamp on to begin heating. *Do not look at the bulb or its reflection!* Do not touch the lamp shade. It can get quite warm!
4. After 5 minutes have elapsed, record temperatures for all the substances.
5. Record temperatures after 10 minutes have elapsed.
6. Turn off the lamp.
7. Record cooling temperatures at 15 and 20 minutes.
8. See FIG. 2-3 for table of previously recorded data.

OBSERVATIONS

How quickly did the temperatures of the sand and dirt rise?
   Which heated faster, the tap or salt water? Why?

QUESTIONS

Sunlight is composed of a fairly large piece of electromagnetic spectrum. We see only the visible portion of this spectrum. What is on "either side" of this visible portion? Which portion is partially filtered by the Earth's atmosphere?
   What role does the ozone layer perform in the atmosphere?
   How is the ozone layer being destroyed? Where is the hole in our atmosphere the largest?

EARTH EVENT

Perform this experiment again, using a 100-watt white lamp to simulate a noon-day summer sun in Southern California. How do these temperatures compare to the ones obtained using the UV lamp?
   As an additional exercise, graph the results using the appropriate scale.

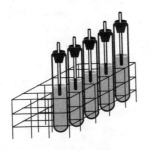

Test tube rack with
five test tubes

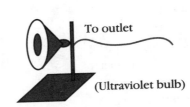

To outlet

(Ultraviolet bulb)

Lamp, with ring stand

2-1   Heating/cooling of actual land forms experiment setup

Substance	Heating/cooling temperatures every 5 minutes (°C)					
	0	Heating	5	10	Cooling	15	20
Sand							
Dirt							
Grass							
Tap water							
Salt water							

2-2 Heating/cooling data table

Substance	Heating/cooling temperatures every 5 minutes (°C)					
	0	Heating	5	10	Cooling	15	20
Sand	27		30	31		30	29
Dirt	28		32	35		34	31.5
Grass	26		29	32		31	29
Tap water	25		26	28		28	28
Salt water	27		28	31		30	30

2-3 Heating/cooling sample data table (UV light)

The ultraviolet sun (heating/cooling of actual land forms)   9

3

The ultraviolet sun (evaporation of moisture from land forms)

How quickly would water evaporate from substances bombarded with light composed mostly of ultraviolet rays vs. white sunlight?

Quite possibly there are planets with atmospheres that filter out less UV light than ours. Our atmosphere has a layer of ozone (triatomic oxygen) in the stratosphere. This helps to filter out most of the infrared and ultraviolet radiation. (However, the portion of the ozone layer over Antarctica now has a hole in it.)

A sun (whose rays are rich in ultraviolet radiation) shining on a planet with the above-mentioned atmosphere will heat the landscapes differently. This heating will change the amounts of any liquid water that may be contained in the ground or vegetation.

PURPOSE

The purpose of this experiment is to observe how much moisture is evaporated from actual samples of land forms using an ultraviolet light. The data here will be compared to that obtained from a white lamp simulating sunlight.

MATERIALS NEEDED

- 1 75-watt UV lamp
- 1 75-watt white lamp
- 2 lamp shields
- 2 ring stands with clamps
- mass/gram balance—triple beam or pan (to 0.01 grams)
- 3 evaporating dishes or small shallow pans
- 10-ml graduated cylinder
- samples of: dry dirt and sand, grass blades (fresh)

- masking tape
- 100 ml of tap water

Note: A glass aquarium is not used because ultraviolet rays cannot travel through glass.

PROCEDURE

1. See FIG. 3-1 for experiment setup.
2. Label three strips of masking tape with sand, dirt, and grass.
3. Tape one to a dish or pan.
4. Weigh each pan to the nearest 0.01 gram. Record this on FIG. 3-2.
5. Partially fill each pan with its respective substance.
6. Weigh each pan again. Record these masses.
7. Carefully measure 2.0 ml of water in the 10- ml graduated cylinder and pour into each pan.
8. Weigh each pan again.
9. Record this mass in FIG. 3-2.
10. Be sure to perform all subtractions in FIG. 3-2.
11. Arrange all pans under the ultraviolet lamp.
12. Be sure the UV lamp is at least 25 cm away from the substances being heated.
13. Turn lamp on to begin heating. *Do not look at the lamp or its reflection!*
   After 24 hours
14. Turn lamp off.
15. Weigh all pans again. Record these masses.
16. Figures 3-3 and 3-4 are data tables of previously recorded data.
17. Figure 3-4 data was obtained using a 100-watt white lamp 25 cm above the substances.

OBSERVATIONS

Which substance lost the most moisture? Why is this?
   What shape did the grass blades take after the heating?
   Which lost more moisture, the sand or the dirt?
   Why was additional water (2.0 ml) poured into each sample?

QUESTIONS

Which Earth land form seems to lose the greatest amount of moisture? Why was this?

EARTH EVENT

Perform this lab again using a white lamp of the same wattage instead of the UV lamp.
   Try a different colored lamp to see if there is any difference between the color of light vs. amount of evaporation.

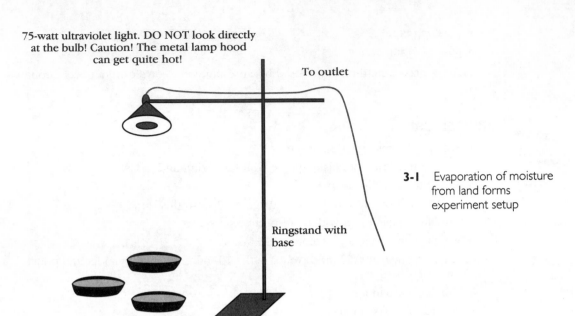

75-watt ultraviolet light. DO NOT look directly at the bulb! Caution! The metal lamp hood can get quite hot!

To outlet

Ringstand with base

3-1 Evaporation of moisture from land forms experiment setup

Evaporating dishes (or shallow plastic pans) Each contains a certain material: sand, grass blades, or dirt.

		Substance		
		Dirt	Sand	Grass
Mass of dish (grams)	A			
Mass of dish with substance (grams)	B			
Mass of "dry" substance (grams)	(B2A)			
Add 2 ml water				
Mass of dish with substance and water (grams)	C			
Mass of "wetted" substance (grams)	(C2A)			
Begin heating . . .				
Mass of dish and substance after 24 hours (grams)	D			
Mass of water evaporated (grams)	(C2D)			

3-2 Evaporation of moisture data table

3-3 Evaporation of moisture sample data table (UV light)

		Substance		
		Dirt	Sand	Grass
Mass of dish (grams)	A	72.90	72.70	72.50
Mass of dish with substance (grams)	B	107.20	124.00	77.10
Mass of "dry" substance (grams)	(B2A)	34.30	51.30	4.60
Add 2 ml water				
Mass of dish with substance and water (grams)	C	109.20	126.00	79.10
Mass of "wetted" substance (grams)	(C2A)	36.30	53.30	6.60
Begin heating . . .				
Mass of dish and substance after 24 hours (grams)	D	106.35	124.00	73.40
Mass of water evaporated (grams)	(C2D)	2.85	2.00	5.70

3-4 Evaporation of moisture sample data table (white lamp)

		Substance		
		Dirt	Sand	Grass
Mass of dish (grams)	A	72.90	72.70	72.50
Mass of dish with substance (grams)	B	107.20	124.00	77.10
Mass of "dry" substance (grams)	(B2A)	34.30	51.30	4.60
Add 2 ml water				
Mass of dish with substance and water (grams)	C	109.20	126.00	79.10
Mass of "wetted" substance (grams)	(C2A)	36.30	53.30	6.60
Begin heating . . .				
Mass of dish and substance after 24 hours (grams)	D	106.60	124.20	73.50
Mass of water evaporated (grams)	(C2D)	2.60	1.80	5.60

4
Heating of land forms by a binary star (blue dwarf, red giant)

On a planet with a red giant/blue dwarf sun system, both suns are rotating on their own axes and revolving around one another. A rather strangely colored pair, they bathe the probably airless landscape with two eerie glows: anti-red and anti-blue shadows are cast from any object blocking the light.

Such an effect has been called the "Flammarion Effect." A French astronomical popularizer (Camille Flammarion) discussed the existence of double stars of different colors and how they would bathe the surface of a planet with their two hues of light.

How would the rock or sand (or similar substance) heat on this surface? What would the temperatures be like just below the surface, 1 to 2 centimeters? Which substance would become hotter with exposure from both suns? The equipment setup here will simulate a "noon hour" from both suns casting their light.

PURPOSE

The purpose of this experiment is to observe the heating temperatures of actual land forms that are heated from models of blue and red suns.

MATERIALS NEEDED

- aquarium
- glass cover
- 4 alcohol thermometers
- 2 trays or pans
- samples of dry sand and small pebbles
- 3 ring stands with clamps
- 3 lamps: 100-watt red, 100-watt blue, 100-watt white (if performed indoors)
- 3 lamp shields
- clock or watch with second hand

PROCEDURE

1. See FIG. 4-1 for experiment setup.
2. Make additional copies if the white lamp is used or the experiment is performed in outside sunlight.
3. Figure 4-2 is a front view of how the thermometers are actually placed on (and in) each substance.
4. Be sure the samples used are clean and dry.
5. Pour enough into each pan or tray to cover the bottom with at least 4 cm of depth.
6. Place both pans inside the aquarium.
7. Record beginning temperatures on FIG. 4-3.
8. Turn lamps on to begin heating.
9. Record temperatures on each thermometer every minute.
10. After 15 minutes, turn lamps off.
11. Let the thermometers cool to reach room temperature before performing the experiment again for another lamp.
12. Discard the used materials in appropriate waste containers.
13. See FIGS. 4-4, 4-5 and 4-6 for previously recorded data.

OBSERVATIONS

How quickly did the surface temperatures for the sand and rock change?
Which substance heated more quickly?
Compare the subsurface temperatures. Did they level off?
Which reading below surface was the warmest? Which was the coolest?
Did the sunlight seem to heat the sand and rock faster than either light? (Remember, they were inside an aquarium. Therefore, there was a "greenhouse" effect.)

QUESTIONS

Obviously, there was an "atmosphere" in the aquarium during the heating. How would the slope of a heating graph appear if the aquarium could be completely airless? How does the atmosphere surrounding the Earth help to regulate temperatures?

EARTH EVENT

Perform this experiment again, but place the aquarium outside on a wood bench on a sunny day. How do your temperatures compare to those in FIG. 4-6? How does time of day affect any heating?

If the experiment is performed indoors, use the 100-watt white lamp. Follow the above procedures.
Make four graphs:
Rock   Surface
Rock   Below surface
Sand   Surface
Sand   Below surface

Label the graphs appropriately using the correct scale. Each graph will have three lines on it representing the data for the three lamps.

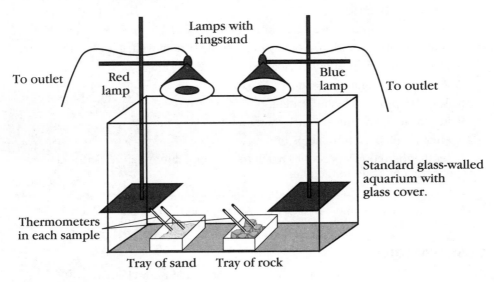

4-1   Binary star heating experiment setup

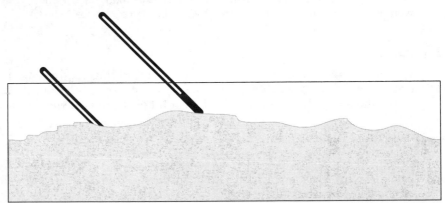

One thermometer must be carefully pushed into the rock or dirt at least 2 cm.

The surface thermometer merely rests on top of the material.

Be sure both thermometers are turned so the readings can be read easily.

4-2   Binary star heating (close-up view)

Heating time in minutes	ROCK temperature (°C)		SAND temperature (°C)	
	Surface	2 cm below	Surface	2 cm below
0				
1				
2				
3				
4				
5				
6				
7				
8				
9				
10				
11				
12				
13				
14				
15				

4-3 Binary star heating data table

Heating time in minutes	ROCK temperature (°C)		SAND temperature (°C)	
	Surface	2 cm below	Surface	2 cm below
0	22	22	24	24
1	24	22	25	25
2	26	22	27	25
3	27	22.5	27.5	26
4	28	23	28	27
5	29	23	29	27
6	30	24	30	27
7	31	24.5	30	28
8	32	25	31	28
9	32	26	31	28
10	33	26	32	29
11	33	27	32	29
12	34	27	33	29
13	35	28	33	30
14	35.5	28.5	33.5	30
15	36	29	34	30

4-4 Binary star heating sample data table (red/blue lamps)

Heating time in minutes	ROCK temperature (°C)		SAND temperature (°C)	
	Surface	2 cm below	Surface	2 cm below
0	27	27	27	27
1	30	27	28	27
2	35	28	28	27
3	36	28	28.5	28
4	38	29	29	28
5	40	30	29	28
6	41	30	29.5	28
7	43	31	30	28.5
8	44	32	30	29
9	45	32	30.5	29
10	45	33	31	29
11	47	34	31	29.5
12	47.5	34.5	31.5	30
13	48	35	32	30
14	49	36	32	30
15	50	36	32	30

4-5 Binary star heating sample data table (white lamp)

Heating time in minutes	ROCK temperature (°C)		SAND temperature (°C)	
	Surface	2 cm below	Surface	2 cm below
0	27	29	26	27
1	32	30	30	28
2	35	30	33	29.5
3	37	32	34	30.5
4	38	32	35	31.5
5	39	33	37	32
6	40	34	38	33
7	41	35	38	34
8	42	35.5	38	34
9	42	36	39	35
10	43	37	40	35
11	44	37	40	36
12	44	38	40.5	36.5
13	44	39	41	37
14	45	39	41.5	37
15	45	40	42	38

4-6 Binary star heating sample data table (real sunlight)

5
Atmospheric heating on Venus— friction from blowing dust

Your first reaction after setting foot on the planet Venus (assuming you're wearing a space suit for the incredible pressure) is that it would be hot, very hot.

How is this intense heating possible? Why is the antisolar point (dark side of Venus) nearly as hot as the subsolar point (sun-facing side)?

You'll also experience winds of a tremendous velocity. With this wind, there will be much flying dust and sand. It is quite possible that friction from this blowing dust and sand is partially responsible for the atmospheric heating.

PURPOSE

The purpose of this experiment is to attempt a verification of one possible reason why the heating of the atmosphere of Venus occurs: by friction from blowing dust and sand.

MATERIALS NEEDED

- aquarium
- towel
- masking tape
- wet/dry vacuum/blower
- vacuum hose with blowing nozzle
- 2 alcohol thermometers
- dry sand
- clock or watch with second hand
- goggles

PROCEDURE

Caution! Wear goggles at all times when operating the blower.

1. See FIG. 5-1 for experiment setup.
2. Make extra copies of the data table, FIG. 5-2.
3. Tape the towel or rag securely to the aquarium glass.
4. Leave an opening at one end for the nozzle to "poke" through into the tank.
5. Do not add any sand at this point.
6. Record the beginning temperatures of each thermometer on FIG. 5-2. They should be at (or near) room temperature (21° Celsius).
7. Turn on the blower. Point the nozzle inside the aquarium, but away from the thermometers.
8. Run the blower for at least 10 minutes.
9. Record the temperatures of each thermometer at the 5- and 10-minute mark.
10. Turn off the blower.
11. The temperatures recorded are used to compare with those obtained when sand is placed in the tank with the blower in operation.
12. Wait several minutes for the temperatures to return to their original (or room) temperatures.
13. Sprinkle at least 50 grams of sand into the tank. Verify that the tape holding the cloth to the tank is secure.
14. Put goggles on.
15. Record beginning temperatures.
16. Turn on the blower. Again, point the nozzle into the tank, but away from the thermometers.
17. Watch the patterns made by the blowing sand. Some sand grains will rest at the bottom; some grains will whirl about. All should be in motion at one time or another.
18. At the 5- and 10-minute mark, record the temperatures.
19. After 10 minutes, turn off the blower. If any sand has escaped from the tank, use the vacuum portion of the wet/dry vacuum to clean up any spills.
20. See FIGS. 5-3 and 5-4 for previously recorded data.

OBSERVATIONS

How did the heating temperatures with sand compare to those without sand?
Why was the blower initially used in the empty tank?
Did the warm motor contribute to the temperature increase? Why or why not?

QUESTIONS

What are some of the other theories of possible sources of heating on Venus? Hint: Research the greenhouse effect by using the increased output of carbon dioxide gas into Earth's atmosphere as the starting point.

EARTH EVENT

How could blowing dust and sand heat the air in certain areas on Earth?
  How do hot, dry, fast moving winds help to spread forest fires?

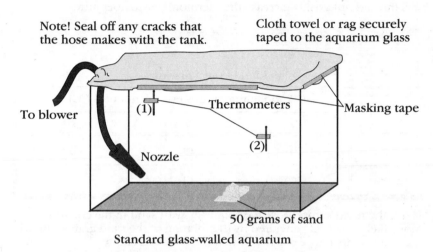

5-1 Atmospheric heating on Venus experiment setup

Thermometer #	Wind temperatures every 5 minutes (°C)		
	0	5	10
1			
2			

5-2 Atmospheric heating on Venus data table

Without sand in the aquarium

Thermometer #	Wind temperatures every 5 minutes (°C)		
	0	5	10
1	26	27	28
2	26	27	28

Note: To ensure that heat from the blowing "wind" did not contribute significantly to the temperature rise, this experiment was performed without any sand in the tank. Although the motor warmed the blowing air, this did not greatly increase the thermometer temperatures.

5-3 Atmospheric heating on Venus sample data table

With sand in the aquarium

Thermometer #	Wind temperatures every 5 minutes (°C)		
	0	5	10
1	26	29	32
2	26	29	32

Here, the temperatures rose more quickly with sand in the aquarium. Most likely, the heat generated by the rubbing of the sand grains caused a greater temperature rise than when the tank was empty.

5-4 Atmospheric heating on Venus sample data table (with sand)

☆ ☆ **FACTOIDS** ☆ ☆

The following facts have been paraphrased from a variety of sources (nearly 400): TV, magazines, research papers, newspapers, and reference books:

- Quite possibly, in the very heart of our Milky Way Galaxy, there exists a black hole. It could be larger than our sun, but not as large as our solar system.
- If a sudden change of climate occurred, wiping out all plant life, all animals (including humans) would become extinct within a few weeks.
- Active life on Earth exists within a narrow range of temperatures (20-120° Fahrenheit). On the other hand, at the center of a black hole, temperatures can be as high as 18 billion degrees Fahrenheit. Empty interstellar space is as cold as -460° Fahrenheit.

☆ ☆ ☆ ☆ ☆ ☆ ☆ ☆ ☆ ☆ ☆ ☆ ☆ ☆ ☆ ☆ ☆ ☆ ☆

6

Binary star (right-angle heating of a planet)

Our Sun, the only star within 4.3 light years, is our source for maintaining life.

Suppose in your travels, you encounter two stars of roughly the same age.

They are several AUs apart and approximately 1 AU from the planet you have landed on. (The distance from Earth to the Sun is 93 million miles. This is known as an astronomical unit or AU.)

They are of the same spectral classification. (The previous experiment used a red/blue sun system.)

Since these suns revolve about one another (and your planet revolves about them) there are two points in their orbits where they are the farthest apart from each other (as viewed from your planet). There are also two points where one is blocking the other. (That is another topic.)

At a "noon-hour" (when both suns are at the highest point overhead for the day) and when these suns are farthest apart from each other (in their orbit around each other during the year), how would their heating together of the planet below compare to one sun?

As an observer on this planet, you would see two suns at right angles from where you're standing in your field of view. Would twice the amount of light mean substances on the planet heat twice as much?

PURPOSE

The purpose of this experiment is to observe how differently substances would heat if two suns (part of a binary sun system) were in the sky above a planet.

MATERIALS NEEDED

- test tube rack
- 5 test tubes
- 5 rubber stoppers (single hole)
- 5 alcohol thermometers

- 2 lamps—each 100-watt white
- 2 lamp shields
- 2 ring stands with clamps
- samples of: dry sand and dirt, grass blades (fresh), tap water, and salt water (3.5% NaCl)
- clock or watch with second hand

PROCEDURE

1. See FIG. 6-1 for experiment setup.
2. See "Experiment preparation techniques" on page xx to make a 3.5% salt solution.
3. Fill all test tubes with the appropriate sample.
4. Be sure to use glycerin or soapy water when inserting the thermometer into the rubber stopper.
5. Insert the thermometer/stopper assembly into the test tube.
6. Place all five test tubes in the front row of the test tube rack.
7. Wait approximately 10 minutes for temperatures to stabilize.
8. Record beginning temperatures on FIG. 6-2.
9. Be sure lamps are 25 cm away from the test tube rack.
10. Turn both lamps on to begin heating and timing.
11. Record temperatures every 5 minutes on FIG. 6-2.
12. At minute 10, turn lamps off.
13. Let the equipment cool to room temperature. It is quite warm.
14. See FIG. 6-3 for previously recorded data for two lamps.
15. Figure 6-4 also contains previously recorded data, but for one lamp.
16. Discard the used materials in the appropriate waste containers.

OBSERVATIONS

Which material heated the fastest? the slowest?

How do these heating temperatures compare to the temperatures in experiment 7?

QUESTIONS

As one sun moves behind another in a double sun system, the light is either completely or partially cut off, depending on the size of the sun doing the blocking. How do you think heating temperatures on a planet with one sun "hiding" the other would compare to two suns heating a planet?

How much would ground wind speed be affected by having two suns heating the Earth instead of one?

Would there be more water vapor, or carbon dioxide, in the atmosphere with heating of the Earth by the two suns?

Is it possible that the wind speed of the jet stream (above Earth) might be greatly affected by extra heating from an additional sun?

EARTH EVENT

Use one lamp for heating to compare these temperatures to the readings obtained in the above experiment. Keep the distance from lamp to substances at 25 centimeters.

Graph the results on 5 separate pieces of graph paper as follows:

sand
dirt
grass
tap water
salt water

Each graph will have two lines on it: one representing two lamps and one for a single lamp. Use the appropriate scale to fit all recorded data.

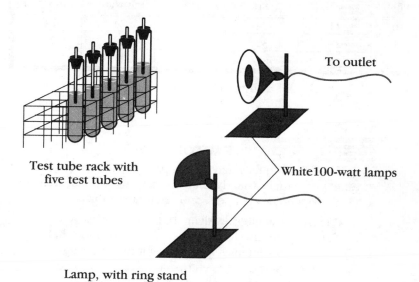

Test tube rack with
five test tubes

To outlet

White 100-watt lamps

Lamp, with ring stand

6-1   Right-angle heating experiment setup

Heating time in minutes	Substance temperature (°C)				
	Sand	Dirt	Grass	Salt water	Tap water
0					
5					
10					

6-2   Right-angle heating data table

Heating time in minutes	Substance temperature (°C)				
	Sand	Dirt	Grass	Salt water	Tap water
0	26	26	28	29	29
5	30	32	34	29	29
10	34	38	37	33.5	33

6-3 Right-angle heating sample data table (2 lamps)

Heating time in minutes	Substance temperature (°C)				
	Sand	Dirt	Grass	Salt water	Tap water
0	24	24	25	24	24
5	27	32	34	28	27
10	30	37	40	31.5	29

6-4 Right-angle heating sample data table (1 lamp)

☆☆ ☆ **FACTOIDS** ☆ ☆

The following facts have been paraphrased from a variety of sources (nearly 400): TV, magazines, research papers, newspapers, and reference books:

- The blue-white star Altair, 16 light years away, spins quite fast, rotating once every six and a half hours. This intense spin flattens it into an "egg-shaped" star due to centripetal forces. Compare this to our sun, which rotates nearly once every month. It is nearly circular.

- Fate of the Earth: after 5 billion years, the Sun will swell into a red giant. The gases in the outer photosphere of our "Sun" will slow the Earth's orbital motion. Earth will spiral inward toward the very hot interior about 10,000 years after the Sun becomes a red giant.

- On Venus, winds blow nearly 220 miles per hour (or 100 meters per second). The fastest human on Earth can run 100 meters in less than 10 seconds.

- The clouds of Venus are concentrated sulfuric acid. Its atmosphere is 96% carbon dioxide.

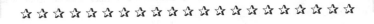

7

Binary star (heating of the Earth)

As two suns of approximately the same size, age and luminosity revolve about one another (similar to the suns in the previous experiment), there are times when one appears to block out the rays of the other (when viewed from a planet orbiting such suns).

Just before one sun hides the other, both appear to be "crowding" one another. Two shadows are cast from an object on a planet blocking the light of this binary pair. As one sun blocks the other, only one shadow is seen cast by this object.

How differently would objects on Earth heat under such sunlight? Would two suns mean rock or sand would heat twice as fast, or twice as hot? If Earth had two suns, would such uneven heating cause different wind and precipitation patterns?

PURPOSE

The purpose of this experiment is to observe the heating of the Earth by using two model suns representing a binary sun system.

MATERIALS NEEDED

- test tube rack
- 5 test tubes
- 5 rubber stoppers (single hole)
- 5 alcohol thermometers
- 2 lamps—each 100-watt white
- 2 lamp shields
- 2 ring stands with clamps
- samples of: dry sand and dirt, grass blades (fresh), tap water, and salt water (3.5% NaCl)
- clock or watch with second hand

PROCEDURE

1. See FIG. 7-1 for experiment setup.
2. See "Experiment preparation techniques" on page xx to prepare a 3.5% salt solution.
3. Fill all test tubes with the appropriate sample.
4. Be sure to use glycerin or soapy water when inserting the thermometer into the rubber stopper.
5. Insert the thermometer/stopper assembly into each test tube.
6. Place all five test tubes in the front row of a test tube rack.
7. Wait approximately 10 minutes for temperatures to stabilize.
8. Record beginning temperatures on FIG. 7-2.
9. The lamps must be 25 cm away from the test tube rack.
10. Be sure that the front lamp is partially blocking the glow of the rear lamp. (Both must still cast their light on the substances being heated.)
11. Turn both lamps on to begin heating and timing.
12. Record temperatures every 5 minutes on FIG. 7-2.
13. At minute 10, turn lamps off.
14. Let the equipment cool to room temperature. It is quite warm.
15. See FIG. 7-3 for previously recorded data for two lamps.
16. Figure 7-4 also contains previously recorded data, but for one lamp.

OBSERVATIONS

Which material heated the fastest? the slowest?

How do these heating temperatures compare to the temperatures in experiment 6?

QUESTIONS

In this experiment the two lamps side-by-side blended together to act approximately like one larger sun. Would one sun of the correct luminosity and mass replacing a binary star give the same heating effects? Explain.

When these two suns revolve around one another, there are two points when one partially or completely blocks the other. As the sun "from behind" emerges, heating temperatures change on the surface of the planet receiving this light. How might the strength of any winds blowing change as well?

EARTH EVENT

Graph the results on 5 separate pieces of graph paper as follows:
    sand
    dirt
    grass
    tap water
    salt water

Each graph will have two lines on it: one representing two lamps and one for a single lamp. (Use the data for the single lamp from the previous experiment.) Use the appropriate scale to fit all recorded data.

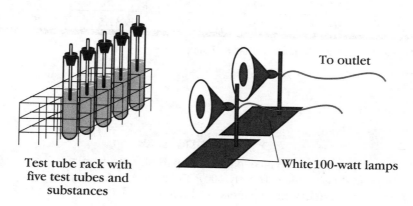

7-1 Heating of Earth experiment setup

Heating time in minutes	Substance temperature (°C)				
	Sand	Dirt	Grass	Salt water	Tap water
0					
5					
10					

7-2 Heating of Earth data table

Heating time in minutes	Substance temperature (°C)				
	Sand	Dirt	Grass	Salt water	Tap water
0	23	25	26.5	23.5	24
5	28	33	36	28	27
10	30.5	38	42	32	30

7-3 Heating of Earth sample data table (2 lamps)

Heating time in minutes	Substance temperature (°C)				
	Sand	Dirt	Grass	Salt water	Tap water
0	24	24	25	24	24
5	27	32	34	28	27
10	30	37	40	31.5	29

7-4 Heating of Earth sample data table (1 lamp)

☆ ☆ FACTOIDS ☆ ☆

The following facts have been paraphrased from a variety of sources (nearly 400): TV, magazines, research papers, newspapers, and reference books:

- It is estimated that more than 800 million tons of sand and soil are washed away to the sea from the continental United States every year.

- There are actually six states of matter:

  1. solid—a piece of gold
  2. liquid—water
  3. gas (non-ionized)—oxygen or nitrogen
  4. gas (ionized)—a neon sign glowing due to an electric charge, for example
  5. plasma (not blood)—atoms of hydrogen fused together (to form helium) at temperatures of 18 million degrees Fahrenheit. Our sun is an example.
  6. "broken nuclei"—protons, electrons, and neutrons torn into fragments themselves. These quarks behave in unimaginable ways. This phase of matter occurs at a mere 18 billion degrees. It's found only in the accretion disk of a "black hole." At this time, there are no known examples.

- A planet (revolving about a star) is defined as a body having a mass less than two times the planet Jupiter's mass. A planet may radiate energy from radioactive elements it contains, but the interior will never become hot enough to have nuclear fusion take place and become a star.

The Earth

The only home to life as we know it, the Earth is in a most fortunate position. It is far enough away from the sun to prevent overheating (and the release of excess carbon dioxide from surface rocks). Yet, it's near enough to stay warm and comfortable.

It has liquid water and nitrogen/oxygen blue skies to sustain temperatures within a range for active life forms, 20° to 120° Fahrenheit. It is teeming with life of all kinds in three different kingdoms: animal, plant, and protist. The life within each phylum and species is as unique as a snowflake.

Is there another planet that harbors life? Is it at our "level" of growth and evolution? Or is it merely waiting for the flashes of unending lightning in some primeval atmosphere to commence the blending of chemicals in their delicate configurations of amino acids in its oceans?

If there is dust in space forming stars (and there are billions of those), there must be planets formed from some of this dust and gas. So far, no planets have been located outside our solar system.

What would astronomers look for to spot a planet? Perhaps they would search for infrared radiation being reflected from an object nearby a star. A planet would reflect some of this infrared radiation into space.

8
Circulatory winds of a non-rotating Earth

Suppose the Earth stopped rotating on its axis. Where could it possibly be the most livable, if only for a short length of time?

Such a non-rotating planet (there could be many others, as well) does exist in our Solar System. Venus is such a planet. It rotates so slowly that it can be considered to be non-rotating. A day on Venus nearly matches its year.

Such slow movement by Venus presents nearly one "side" to the Sun at all times. This is known as the subsolar point. The other side of Venus is the antisolar point.

The heating of its surface produces simple convection cells of enormous size. Rising air at Venus' equator travels to both its poles where it sinks and makes its way back to the equatorial regions.

No liquid oceans have yet been detected on Venus; they are probably absent due to the tremendous atmospheric pressure. It is a planet with thermal runaway temperatures. Blowing sand and dust, excess carbon dioxide, and several other factors may be responsible (in whole or in part) for the heating of Venus.

Would the surface of Earth heat the same way? This experiment is a model to demonstrate this convection cycle.

PURPOSE

The purpose of this lab is to build and operate a simple model that shows the approximate direction a non-rotating planet Earth's winds would travel.

MATERIALS NEEDED

- aquarium
- glass cover
- 6 alcohol thermometers
- masking tape
- 2 shallow pans or bowls
- salt water (3.5% NaCl)
- bunsen burner or alcohol burner

- goggles
- 250-ml glass beaker
- ice cubes
- 100-watt white lamp
- 1 lamp shield
- 1 ring stand with clamp
- dry dirt—to fill one side of the aquarium
- clock or watch with second hand

PROCEDURE

1. See FIG. 8-1 for experiment setup.
2. See "Experiment preparation techniques" on page xx to prepare a 3.5 % NaCl solution.
3. Be sure the dirt used is dry.
4. Place a mound of dirt in one end of the tank as shown in FIG. 8-1.
5. Wear goggles when using the alcohol or bunsen burner.
6. Using approximately 100 ml of the prepared 3.5% NaCl water, gently warm it to approximately 30° Celsius in a glass beaker over a bunsen burner. This is the "ocean temperature" at the equator.
7. Pour this heated salt water into a pan/bowl.
8. The pan of salt water must be placed at the base of the dirt mound.
9. Place a thermometer in the "ocean" water.
10. Place a pan of ice cubes at the top of the dirt mound.
11. Cover the aquarium with the glass cover. It is not necessary to tape the cover to the tank.
12. Be sure the lamp is at least 25 cm away from the side glass wall of the tank.
13. The lamp must face the dirt "mountain" as shown in FIG. 8-1.
14. Record all beginning temperatures on FIG. 8-2. Note that the water temperatures are recorded separately.
15. Turn lamp on to begin heating and timing.
16. Every 5 minutes record all temperatures.
17. At minute 20, turn lamp off. Let it cool to room temperature. It can be quite warm.
18. See FIG. 8-3 for previously recorded data.
19. Discard used materials in the appropriate waste containers.

OBSERVATIONS

Why were trays of water and ice used? How did they assist in the formation of the convection cycle?

Using FIG. 8-3, the data indicates a reverse flow. That is, the warm air is traveling up to the tray of ice, then near the top of the tank, back to the pan of water. Why is this?

How does your recorded data compare to FIG. 8-3?

Does this model effectively explain a non-rotational planet being heated? Why or why not?

QUESTIONS

Venus appears to be a non-rotational planet. That is, its day nearly equals its year. What sort of convection cycle would form on the side facing the sun? Away from the sun?

EARTH EVENT

Perform the experiment again, but switch the location of the ice with the water. How does this affect the direction of the convection cycle? Would the position of the lamp have to be changed as well? (Try placing the light above the aquarium over the "top" of the dirt hill.)

Suggestion: Try placing a thermometer into the dirt at some point in the aquarium. Measure the temperature changes at this location. How does location of this thermometer affect its heating rate by the lamp?

Standard glass-walled aquarium with glass cover
Thermometers are taped to the inside front wall
with masking tape.

Ice cubes in bowl or beaker

Alcohol thermometer

To outlet

Mound of dirt in one end of the tank

Bowl of warm salt water (30° C)

100-watt lamp

8-1 Circulatory winds experiment setup

Thermometer #	Heating temperatures every 5 minutes (°C)				
	0	5	10	15	20
1					
2					
3					
4					
5					
6					

Beginning water temperature (°C)	
Ending water temperature (°C)	

8-2 Circulatory winds data table

Thermometer #	Heating temperatures every 5 minutes (°C)				
	0	5	10	15	20
1	25	30	32	33	33
2	26	27	28	29	29
3	26	27	28	28	28
4	24	24	25	25	25
5	25	27	28	28	29
6	26	28	29	30	30

Beginning water temperature (°C)	30
Ending water temperature (°C)	29

8-3 Circulatory winds sample data table

9
Flat Earth weather

At one time, people believed the Earth to be flat. Unfortunately, a tiny minority still clings to that notion. For a moment, assume they are correct. What would the weather be like on a flat Earth?

How would shadow lengths (from objects blocking the sunlight) appear to observers across this "piece" of flat land? How could rotation of such a place occur? What would the shape of the Earth's shadow appear to be during the Moon's phases or eclipses?

Our questions range from the sensible (above) to the ridiculous. What is "underneath" our flat planet? Why would the oceans stay in one place and not tumble off the "edges?"

How would the Earth land and water forms heat? Would there be any circulatory patterns? For a wind to blow, there must be a place of cooling as well as heating.

Flat Earth believers have difficulty in explaining the existence of the Coriolis force (the deflection of winds due to Earth rotation).

PURPOSE

The purpose of this experiment is to build and operate a simple model that shows how a flat model Earth would heat and cool.

MATERIALS NEEDED

- aquarium
- glass cover
- 2 shallow pans
- ice cubes
- bunsen burner or alcohol
- 500-ml glass beaker
- goggles
- salt water (3.5% NaCl)
- 6 alcohol thermometers
- 100-watt white lamp
- 1 lamp shield
- 1 ring stand with clamp

- dry dirt (or sand)—to fill aquarium approximately one-third full
- clock or watch with second hand

PROCEDURE

1. See FIG. 9-1 for experiment setup.
2. Use enough dry dirt (or sand) in the tank to provide at least 3 inches (7.6 cm) of depth.
3. Tape all thermometers to the inside front wall of the aquarium with masking tape.
4. See "Experiment preparation techniques" on page xx to prepare a 100 ml 3.5% NaCl water solution.
5. Wear goggles when using the alcohol or bunsen burner.
6. Heat this water (gently) to approximately 30° Celsius in a 500-ml glass beaker.
7. Fill a shallow pan with this "ocean."
8. Fill two pans with ice cubes. Place one pan at each end of the tank.

   If performed outdoors

   a. Be sure it is a clear and calm, sunny day. A windy day might blow objects at the experiment setup, possibly damaging it.

   b. Place the aquarium on a wood table or desk. This will reduce any influences from the ground as well as provide support for the tank's increased mass.

   c. Place the glass cover over the tank. Use masking tape to hold the cover securely.

   d. Be sure to perform this experiment between the hours of 11 a.m. and 2 p.m.

   If performed indoors

   a. The lamp distance to the side glass is 50 cm for any "sunrise" or "sunset" temperatures. (This position will ensure that indirect heating will be approximately equal at both ends of the tank.)

   b. The lamp can be oriented at any other angle to simulate the position of the sun over the Earth. Keep the lamp at least 25 cm away from the aquarium during the heating if other positions are used.

   Continued procedure for either indoor or outside setup

9. Record all beginning *heating* temperatures on FIG. 9-2.
10. Place the apparatus outside or turn lamp on to begin heating.
11. Record temperatures every 5 minutes until minute 15.
12. Bring the aquarium back indoors or turn lamp off to begin cooling.
13. Record all beginning *cooling* temperatures on FIG. 9-3.
14. Record temperatures every 5 minutes until minute 15.
15. Figures 9-4 and 9-5 (of previously recorded data) were made outside on a sunny July day, at approximately 1 pm.
16. Discard the used materials in the appropriate waste containers.

OBSERVATIONS

Refer to FIG. 9-4. How did all heating temperatures on each thermometer compare (that is, #4 with #2, and #5 with #1)? Why would the heating occur in this fashion? How does your data compare with this?

Refer to FIG. 9-5. The cooling temperatures were fairly consistent throughout the tank. Why did #6 appear to cool faster than #3?

QUESTIONS

As a ship "disappears" over the horizon, it does so from the bottom to the top (from the hull to the wheel house). How would a ship disappear on a flat Earth?

Eratosthenes was able to calculate (with remarkable precision) the circumference of the Earth. Approximately 2,000 years ago, he correctly concluded that the Earth was spherical. (From a purist's point of view, the Earth is actually slightly "squashed" at its poles because of its spin.) What man-made fixture in ancient Syene (near present-day Abu Simbel), Egypt, was he aware of that allowed him to perform these calculations?

EARTH EVENT

Graph your data on two graphs:
      Heating temperature vs. time
      Cooling temperature vs. time
      What is the slope of all six lines?
      Suggestion: Place a thermometer into the "ocean" to measure its heating temperatures. How do these readings compare to the temperatures of the "atmosphere?"

Standard glass-walled aquarium with glass cover
Thermometers are taped to the inside front wall
of the aquarium.

Note that this experiment can also be performed outdoors on a sunny day. For best results, use the hours between 11 am to 2 pm, local time. Here, the lamp at this angle represents a "sunrise" for the entire planet (shadow lengths would be the same length at any time of day on a flat planet).

9-1   Flat Earth weather experiment setup

Thermometer #	Heating temperatures every 5 minutes (°C)			
	0	5	10	15
1				
2				
3				
4				
5				
6				

9-2 Flat Earth weather data table (heating)

Thermometer #	Cooling temperatures every 5 minutes (°C)			
	0	5	10	15
1				
2				
3				
4				
5				
6				

9-3 Flat Earth weather data table (cooling)

Thermometer #	Heating temperatures every 5 minutes (°C)			
	0	5	10	15
1	23	30	32	32
2	23	31	33	34
3	23	32	34	35
4	23	31	33	34
5	23	30	32	33
6	23	31	33	35

9-4 Flat Earth weather sample data table (heating)

Thermometer #	Cooling temperatures every 5 minutes (°C)			
	0	5	10	15
1	30	28	26	24
2	32	29	27	25
3	33	29	28	27
4	32	29	27	25
5	30	28	26	24
6	32	29	26	23

9-5 Flat Earth weather sample data table (cooling)

10
Earth without oceans

Bodies of water act as "buffers" to prevent excessive temperature extremes on land.

On a typical summer day in California (if there is such a day), with the cooling winds blowing in from the Pacific Ocean, San Franciscans stay quite cool at work or play.

However, just 100 miles east in Sacramento, air conditioners click on as temperatures soar into the baking realms of triple-digit heat.

Land and water working together stabilize temperatures along California's or any coastline.

How would the heating temperatures of land on a planet without oceans compare to a world with oceans?

Since land heats and cools more rapidly than water, it is possible that temperature extremes would occur during the day and night.

There would be no onshore breezes or offshore winds that reverse themselves by day and night to temper such extremes.

PURPOSE

The purpose of this experiment is to demonstrate a model of Earth without oceans.

MATERIALS NEEDED

- aquarium
- glass cover
- 7 alcohol thermometers
- masking tape
- 100-watt white lamp
- 1 lamp shield
- 1 ring stand with clamp
- 3 shallow pans
- dry dirt and small pebbles
- salt water (3.5% NaCl)
- clock or watch with second hand

PROCEDURE
Without oceans

1. See FIG. 10-1 for experiment setup.
2. Fill a pan or shallow cardboard box to nearly full with samples of dry rock and sand.
3. Place two thermometers on top of the substances.
4. Mount the other five thermometers to the inside front wall of the aquarium with masking tape.
5. The lamp must be at least 25 cm away from the top of the tank. This will simulate a "noon-hour" Southern California sun on a clear day.
6. Record beginning temperatures on FIG. 10-2 (without-oceans table).
7. Turn lamp on to begin heating and timing.
8. Record heating temperatures at minutes 5 and 10 on FIG. 10-2.
9. At minute 10, turn the lamp off.
10. Record cooling temperatures at minutes 15 and 20.

With oceans

1. See FIG. 10-3 for experiment setup.
2. See "Experiment preparation techniques" on page xx to make a 3.5% salt solution.
3. Fill two shallow pans with tap or salt water (3.5% NaCl).
4. Place one pan of water at each end of the aquarium.
5. Record all beginning temperatures on FIG. 10-4.
6. Turn lamp on to begin heating and timing.
7. Record heating temperatures at minutes 5 and 10 on FIG. 10-4.
8. At minute 10, turn the lamp off.
9. Record cooling temperatures at minutes 15 and 20.
10. See FIGS. 10-5 and 10-6 for previously recorded data.
11. Discard the used materials in the appropriate waste containers.

OBSERVATIONS

Refer to FIGS. 10-5 and 10-6. The temperatures in the "non-ocean" tank seemed to heat faster, but cool more slowly, than in the "ocean-filled" tank. What role did the water play in stabilizing the temperatures?

How does your data compare to FIGS. 10-5 and 10-6? Would the heating temperatures for both situations also depend on the color of the rock or sand used?

QUESTIONS

Since the Moon has no atmosphere (due to its weak gravitational pull) it is heated quite strongly by the sun on the sunny side. On the "dark side," bitterly cold temperatures can be found. Assuming an ocean could exist on the Moon, how might this affect these heating and cooling temperatures?

EARTH EVENT

If the amounts of rock and sand were decreased, but the amount of water used increased, how might this affect the recorded temperatures? Try it!

Graph the data you've recorded onto two sheets of graph paper:

With oceans   All 7 thermometer readings
Without oceans   All 7 readings

How do the heating/cooling slopes of each graph compare to each other? Be sure to graph temperature vs. time, using the appropriate scale.

Suggestion: Try using rock of different colors and compositions.

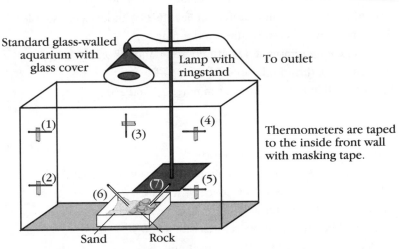

10-1   Earth without oceans experiment setup

Thermometer #	Without "oceans" Heating/cooling temperatures every 5 minutes (°C)					
	0		5	10		15	20
1							
2							
3							
4							
5							
6							
7							

10-2   Earth without oceans data table

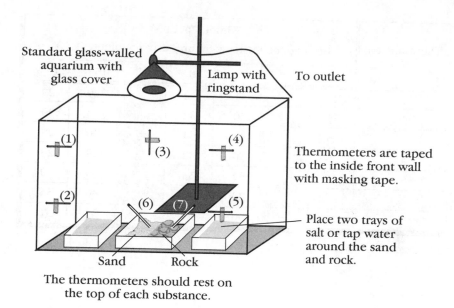

Standard glass-walled aquarium with glass cover

Lamp with ringstand

To outlet

(1)
(3)
(4)
(2)
(6)
(7)
(5)

Thermometers are taped to the inside front wall with masking tape.

Place two trays of salt or tap water around the sand and rock.

Sand   Rock

The thermometers should rest on the top of each substance.

10-3 Earth with oceans experiment setup

Thermometer #	With "oceans" Heating/cooling temperatures every 5 minutes (°C)					
	0	Heating	5	10	Cooling	15	20
1							
2							
3							
4							
5							
6							
7							

10-4 Earth with oceans data table

Thermometer #	Without "oceans" Heating/cooling temperatures every 5 minutes (°C)						
	0		5	10		15	20
1	25		31	32		29	29
2	25		30	32		30	29
3	25	Heating	32	34	Cooling	30	29
4	25		30	32		29	28
5	25		32	33		30	29
6	24		29	35		36	34
7	23		30	35		33	31

10-5   Earth without oceans sample data table

Thermometer #	With "oceans" Heating/cooling temperatures every 5 minutes (°C)						
	0		5	10		15	20
1	27		31	33		29	28
2	27		31	32		29	28
3	26	Heating	31	33	Cooling	29	28
4	26		31	32		29	28
5	27		31	32		29	28
6	29		29.5	31		31	31
7	27		27.5	28		28	28

10-6   Earth with oceans sample data table

II

Earth to sun distance (2 or more AUs)

Here, two methods are used to show how the temperatures on the planet Earth might differ if the Sun were at different distances. Of course, the model in method I is merely measuring the air temperature around the thermometers, but the idea here is to show that when Earth/Sun distance is twice the normal distance, the heating temperatures will be lower.

Since the Sun's illumination is spread over four times the area on the Earth, the heating will be less (from pole to pole). How much less? Will it be half of the observed temperatures at the original (1 AU distance)?

Method II is inferring that the further away the planet is from its sun, the cooler its average stabilized temperature will be.

The formula to calculate a theoretical temperature for each model planet 2, 3, and 4 AU from its sun is provided. This calculation will be compared to the observed temperatures made in Method II.

PURPOSE

The purpose of this experiment (Method I) is to show how much less heating on an Earth twice the distance from the Sun would occur.

The purpose of Method II is to show how heating might occur on planets three or four times as far from the sun as Earth. We will construct a graph showing such heating.

MATERIALS NEEDED
Method I

- large world globe or sphere of a suitable size with stand
- 7 alcohol thermometers
- one meter stick
- masking tape
- 100-watt white lamp
- 1 lamp shield
- 1 ring stand with clamp
- clock or watch with second hand

Method II

- 1 meter stick
- 4 test tubes
- 4 rubber stoppers (single hole)
- 4 alcohol thermometers
- 100-watt white lamp
- 1 lamp shield
- clock or watch with second hand

PROCEDURE
Method I

1. See FIG. 11-1 for experiment setup.
2. Tape the seven thermometers to the latitudes indicated in FIG. 11-1.
3. Place the lamp at the same height as the equator indicated on the globe.

   For 2 AU distance
4. Be sure the lamp is 1 meter away from the globe. This distance represents the Earth/Sun distance of 2 Astronomical Units. (1 AU is equal to approximately 93 million miles.)
5. Record beginning temperatures on FIG. 11-2.
6. Turn lamp on to begin heating and timing.
7. Record heating temperatures at the 5 and 10 minute mark.
8. After 10 minutes, turn the lamp off.
9. Let the thermometer readings return to room temperature.

   For 1 AU distance
10. Move the lamp to a 50 cm (one half meter) distance from the globe.
11. Record beginning temperatures on FIG. 11-3.
12. Turn lamp on to begin heating and timing.
13. After 10 minutes, turn the lamp off.
14. Let the apparatus cool to room temperature. It is quite warm!
15. See FIGS. 11-4 and 11-5 for previously recorded data.

Method II

1. See FIG. 11-6 for experiment setup.
2. Place one end of the meterstick at the lamp shield.
3. Use glycerin or soapy water to slide a rubber stopper onto each thermometer.
4. Slide the stopper/thermometer onto a clean and dry test tube. Be sure the seal is tight.

5. Let all thermometers reach room temperature if they have been used in a previous experiment.

6. Record beginning temperatures on FIG. 11-7 in the box labeled "(A) Beginning temperature."

7. Turn lamp on to begin heating and timing.

8. The temperature readings on all thermometers should stabilize within 10 to 20 minutes.

9. After the readings stabilize, record each on FIG. 11-7 in the box labeled "(B) Stabilized temperature."

10. Turn the lamp off. Let it cool to room temperature.

11. Calculate and record the observed temperature change in FIG. 11-7.

12. Using FIG. 11-8, calculate the theoretical temperature changes.

13. The observed temperature at 1 AU (25 cm) is used as the base to predict the theoretical temperatures.

14. See FIG. 11-9 for previously recorded data and predicted temperature changes.

OBSERVATIONS
Method I

Which latitude received the most direct light at 2 AU? at 1 AU?

How much heating did the two poles undergo? Was it significantly less at the 2 AU position?

Method II

Which "planet" received the most light? How did the temperatures compare at 1 AU to the rest of the "planets?"

At the 4 AU distance, the light is so spread out, the temperatures do not change as drastically as some of the other distances. What would the temperatures possibly be if a test tube/thermometer were placed at 5 AU? 10 AU?

QUESTIONS

Graph the results for the first method (all 7 latitude temperatures). How do the slopes of the pole temperatures compare to the equatorial readings?

EARTH EVENT

Compare the insolation (INcoming SOLar radiATION) of the Earth with that of the other planets. Some of the other planets have atmospheres, enough to become warm from the distant sunlight. Why are the planet surface temperatures so different than Earth's?

Method 1

Large model globe of the Earth; 7 ALCOHOL thermometers are taped at the following latitudes: North Pole; 60° N.; 30° N.; 0° (or equator); 30° S.; 60° S.; and the South Pole.

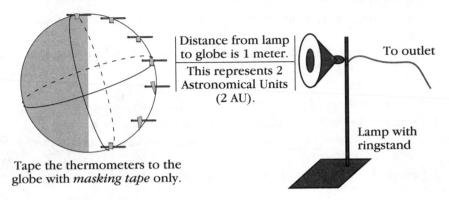

Distance from lamp to globe is 1 meter.

This represents 2 Astronomical Units (2 AU).

To outlet

Lamp with ringstand

Tape the thermometers to the globe with *masking tape* only.

11-1   Earth to sun distance experiment setup (Method 1)

Latitude position	Heating temperatures every 5 minutes (°C)		
	0	5	10
North Pole			
60° North			
30° North			
Equator (0°)			
30° South			
60° South			
South Pole			

Earth to sun distance:

2 AU

11-2   Earth to sun distance data table (2 AU)

Latitude position	Heating temperatures every 5 minutes (°C)		
	0	5	10
North Pole			
60° North			
30° North			
Equator (0°)			
30° South			
60° South			
South Pole			

Earth to sun distance: 1 AU

11-3 Earth to sun distance data table (1 AU)

Latitude position	Heating temperatures every 5 minutes (°C)		
	0	5	10
North Pole	25	27	28
60° North	25	29	29
30° North	25	29	30
Equator (0°)	25	27	28
30° South	25	27	27
60° South	24	25	25
South Pole	24	25	25

Earth to sun distance: 2 AU

11-4 Method I, sample temperatures for 2 AU

Latitude position	Heating temperatures every 5 minutes (°C)		
	0	5	10
North Pole	25	26	27
60° North	25	28	28
30° North	25	32	34
Equator (0°)	25	39	41
30° South	25	35	36
60° South	24	27	28
South Pole	24	26	26

Earth to sun distance: 1 AU

11-5 Method I, sample temperatures for 1 AU

Method 2

Caution! Use soapy water or glycerin in sliding the rubber stopper onto thermometer. Use only alcohol thermometers and be sure readings are visible befor the experiment begins.

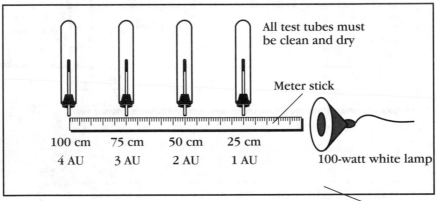

All test tubes must be clean and dry

Meter stick

| 100 cm | 75 cm | 50 cm | 25 cm |
| 4 AU | 3 AU | 2 AU | 1 AU |

100-watt white lamp

This drawing has the student looking down at the experiment setup from above.

Desk or table

11-6 Earth to sun distance experiment setup (Method II)

Thermometer #	A	B	A2B	From FIG. 11-8
	Beginning temperature (°C)	Stabilized temperature (°C)	Temperature change (°C)	Theoretical temperature change (°C)
1 (25 cm)				
2 (50 cm)				
3 (75 cm)				
4 (100 cm)				

11-7 Earth to sun distance data table

Theoretical temperature calculations:

1. Using the observed temperature change for the thermometer closest to the lamp (1 AU525 cm), you can now calculate what the predicted temperature should be for the other thermometers.

$$\text{Theoretical temperature change} = \frac{\text{Observed temperature change at 1 AU}}{d^2}$$

"d" is the distance in AU from the lamp, 2, 3, and 4. Square these values. Divide the observed temperature change by this squared value. Round off the answer to the nearest tenth.

2. Write this theoretical temperature change in the space available in FIG. 11-7.

3. Temperature change should decrease with the square of the distance. At 2 AU, the temperature change should be one-fourth as much, rather than one-half as much. At 3 AU and 4 AU, the change is one-ninth and one-sixteenth as much, respectively, as compared to the distance of 1 AU.

11-8 Earth to sun distance theoretical temperatures

Thermometer #	A Beginning temperature (°C)	B Stabilized temperature (°C)	A2B Temperature change (°C)	From FIG. 11-8 Theoretical temperature change (°C)
1 (25 cm)	24	36.5	12.5	
2 (50 cm)	24	30.5	6.5	3.1
3 (75 cm)	24	26.5	2.5	1.4
4 (100 cm)	24	25	1	0.78

11-9 Earth to sun distance sample data table

The Atmosphere

In the exploration of our galaxy, there are a multitude of planets. Each has its own atmosphere: airless, oxygen/nitrogen, carbon dioxide, methane, hydrogen/helium, or some other mixture of gases.

Each different atmosphere presents a myriad of possibilities. It must be breathable to any inhabitants in order to sustain life. It might be poisonous to many visitors (noxious to some, at least). What is rainfall like, if it exists? Do the inhabitants of a large, gaseous ball like Jupiter float and slither in the less dense parts of their sky?

Does lightning play a part in reforestation of other planets as well? Is the planet in its formative stages of life where electrical discharges manufacture a "goo," the stuff that precedes life?

These questions, and more, are left to the reader. The brilliant minds of science fiction writers may be more correct in their writings than most suspect, for what we can visualize as physically possible within our physical laws most likely is occurring (or has occurred) on some planet somewhere.

These next few experiments require the making of a carbon dioxide atmosphere with nitrogen. The preparation of this atmosphere is an experiment in itself.

12
Rain in a CO$_2$/N$_2$ atmosphere

On a planet with mostly carbon dioxide in its atmosphere (Earth's is just a fraction), how much rain would actually fall?

Earth's atmosphere is nitrogen (78%), oxygen (21%), and a few other trace gases. Two of these trace gases are water vapor and carbon dioxide.

Perhaps water evaporates faster and condenses faster within an atmosphere comprised mainly of carbon dioxide. Is it possible that the pressure of such an atmosphere affects evaporation and condensation?

How does the "normal" pressure of such an atmosphere compare to our normal sea level pressure (29.92 in. Hg or 14.7 lbs/psi)?

The model sun used in this experiment will simulate a noon-day sun of Southern California during a typical summer day.

PURPOSE

The purpose of this experiment is to create a model carbon dioxide/nitrogen atmosphere. The model will attempt to influence the evaporation and subsequent condensation of water in this atmosphere.

MATERIALS NEEDED
- aquarium
- glass cover
- masking tape
- 6 wire mesh heating screens
- 1 candle
- 1 candle holder
- 1 shallow pan
- tap water
- 1 alcohol thermometer
- 1 100-watt white lamp
- 1 lamp shield
- 1 ring stand with clamp
- centimeter ruler
- goggles

PROCEDURE

Caution! The metal heating screens, lamp, and shield will become hot. Always wear goggles when using an open flame.

For prepared nitrogen/carbon dioxide atmosphere

1. See FIG. 12-1 for experiment setup.
2. Make extra copies of FIG. 12-2 for the other atmospheres used.
3. See "Experiment Preparation Techniques" on page xix to set up for a carbon dioxide atmosphere.
4. Be sure the lamp is at least 25 cm away from the top of the aquarium. This will prevent overheating and possible cracking of the glass cover.
5. Fill a shallow pan or tray with 2.0 cm of room temperature tap water.
6. Accurately measure the depth of this water on a level surface with a ruler.
7. Place the pan inside the tank.
8. Light the candle inside the tank.
9. Place the heating screens over the candle.
10. Turn the lamp on to begin heating.
11. Record the beginning temperature on FIG. 12-2.
12. Seal the lid to the tank with masking tape strips.
13. Heat the tank for 24 hours.

    After 24 hours

14. Large drops of condensed water should be on the glass cover away from the lamp light.
15. Record the ending temperature on FIG. 12-2.
16. Turn the lamp off.
17. Carefully remove the masking tape strips from the glass cover. Open the aquarium. Carefully remove the pan or tray. Set the pan on a level surface. Accurately measure the depth of the remaining water.
18. Record this final height of water on FIG. 12-2.
19. Calculate the amount of "rain" on FIG. 12-2.
20. See FIG. 12-3 for previously recorded data using the carbon dioxide atmosphere.
21. Pour out the condensed water inside the tank. Dry the tank thoroughly.

For nitrogen/oxygen atmosphere — "air"

Perform this experiment again, using a sealed tank with air. Use the previous steps for heating and recording data. See FIG. 12-4 for previously recorded data for nitrogen/oxygen atmosphere.

OBSERVATIONS

How do the ending temperatures for both atmospheres compare to each other? Which one is warmer?

Which atmosphere had the most "rain" fall in it? Explain.

QUESTIONS

Mars has a mostly carbon dioxide atmosphere. Why isn't there a great deal of precipitation falling on the planet?

If Earth's atmosphere had more water vapor, would there be more rainfall? Explain.

EARTH EVENT

Obtain a world map of the Earth. Laminate it with plastic. Draw the location of each biome.

Where does the greatest amount of rainfall occur on this planet? In what area does the least amount of rain fall over?

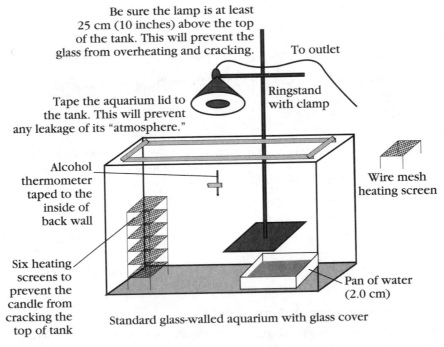

Be sure the lamp is at least 25 cm (10 inches) above the top of the tank. This will prevent the glass from overheating and cracking.

To outlet

Tape the aquarium lid to the tank. This will prevent any leakage of its "atmosphere."

Ringstand with clamp

Alcohol thermometer taped to the inside of back wall

Wire mesh heating screen

Six heating screens to prevent the candle from cracking the top of tank

Pan of water (2.0 cm)

Standard glass-walled aquarium with glass cover

12-1 Rain in a CO_2 atmosphere experiment setup

Beginning temperature	Ending temperature	Initial height of water	Final height of water	Amount of "rain"
(°C)	(°C)	(A)	(B)	(A−B)
		2.0 cm		
Atmosphere used (circle one): N₂/O₂ N₂/CO₂				

12-2   Rain in a CO_2 atmosphere data table

Beginning temperature	Ending temperature	Initial height of water	Final height of water	Amount of "rain"
(°C)	(°C)	(A)	(B)	(A−B)
27.5°	29.5°	2.0 cm	1.2 cm	0.80 cm
Atmosphere used (circle one): N₂/O₂ (N₂/CO₂)				

12-3   Rain in a CO_2 sample data table (N_2/O_2)

Beginning temperature	Ending temperature	Initial height of water	Final height of water	Amount of "rain"
(°C)	(°C)	(A)	(B)	(A−B)
27.5°	27°	2.0 cm	1.5 cm	0.5 cm
Atmosphere used (circle one): (N₂/O₂) N₂/CO₂				

12-4   Rain in a CO_2 atmosphere sample data table (N_2/O_2)

13

Heating/cooling of land with a green sky

Our sky is blue because gaseous molecules of a certain size reflect the visible blue spectrum of light emanating from the Sun.

Air is a mixture of a number of gases: most notably nitrogen and oxygen. It is the size of these molecules that reflects and refracts the blue frequencies of sunlight. This light is scattered throughout the atmosphere.

As one travels into outer space, the sky gradually turns to a black color. (There are very few air molecules 110 miles up where the space shuttle orbits, hence astronauts see a black sky further away from the Earth.)

The blue region visible to the shuttle personnel, incidentally, is due to the light reflecting off the oceans.

Would plants grow in a sunlight filtering through a green sky here on Earth? Perhaps you can design an experiment to try to answer this question.

PURPOSE

The purpose of this experiment is to demonstrate the heating and cooling of actual land forms of a model Earth using a green sky.

MATERIALS NEEDED

- aquarium
- glass cover
- test tube rack
- 5 test tubes
- 5 rubber stoppers (single hole)
- 5 alcohol thermometers
- 3 "overhead transparency" green plastic sheets
- masking tape
- 1 100-watt white lamp
- 1 lamp shield
- 1 ring stand with clamp
- samples of: dry sand and dirt, grass blades (fresh), tap water, and salt water (3.5% NaCl)

PROCEDURE

1. See FIG. 13-1 for experiment setup.
2. See "Experiment preparation techniques" on page xx for instructions on making a 3.5% salt solution.
3. Fill the five test tubes approximately halfway, one each with sand, dirt, grass, tap water, and salt water (3.5% NaCl).
4. Slide a thermometer into a rubber stopper using glycerin or soapy water.
5. Carefully, place each thermometer/stopper into each test tube.
6. Fill the front portion of a test tube rack with the prepared test tubes.
7. Place the rack into the aquarium.
8. Cover the tank with the glass cover. It is not necessary to seal the aquarium.
9. Be sure the lamp is 25 cm away from the aquarium.
10. Tape the 3 green transparencies to the side of the tank exposed to the light.
11. Record beginning temperatures on FIG. 13-2.
12. Turn lamp on to begin heating and timing.
13. Record heating temperatures at minutes 5 and 10 on FIG. 13-2.
14. Turn lamp off at minute 10.
15. Record cooling temperatures at minutes 15 and 20 on FIG. 13-2.
16. See FIG. 13-3 for previously recorded data for a "green" sky.
17. See FIG. 13-4 for previously recorded data for a "clear" sky.
18. Discard the used materials in the appropriate waste containers.

OBSERVATIONS

How quickly did the sand and dirt heat, compared to each other?
    Which substance heated the greatest amount? Why?
    How did the temperatures of the salt and tap water compare?

QUESTIONS

Would a different colored sky inhibit the heating effects of a sun such as ours? Explain.

    How is the smoke from volcanic eruptions affecting the heating temperatures on this planet?

    Would such a smoke-filled sky allow only certain frequencies of light to pass through while absorbing others? What effects might this have on animal or plant life at the surface?

EARTH EVENT

Repeat the experiment, without using the "green sky" filter. Try using a red or blue lamp with the green sky.

    Graph the results on different sheets of graph paper. Be sure to use the appropriate scale to fit all temperatures recorded. Your graph will have five lines on it. Each line represents a different substance used in the test tubes.

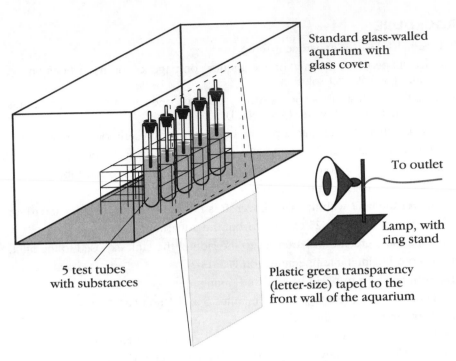

13-1 Heating/cooling of land with a green sky experiment setup

Substance	Heating/cooling temperatures every 5 minutes (°C)						
	0	Heating	5	10	Cooling	15	20
Sand							
Dirt							
Grass							
Tap water							
Salt water							

13-2 Heating/cooling data table

Substance	Heating/cooling temperatures every 5 minutes (°C)					
	0	Heating	5	10	Cooling	15	20
Sand	25		26	27		26.5	26
Dirt	25		26.5	28		27.5	27
Grass	25		28	30.5		29	27
Tap water	25		27	28		27.5	27
Salt water	25		27	28		27	27

13-3 Heating/cooling sample data table (green sky)

Substance	Heating/cooling temperatures every 5 minutes (°C)					
	0	Heating	5	10	Cooling	15	20
Sand	28		32	36		33	31
Dirt	28		39	46		39	34
Grass	25		37	42		35	30
Tap water	22		27	30		29	27
Salt water	24		30	35		33	31

13-4 Heating/cooling sample data table (clear sky)

14

Evaporation of water vapor from land with a CO_2/N_2 atmosphere

How would the amount of carbon dioxide in an atmosphere on another planet affect any evaporation of water from plant life, sand, or soil?

Assuming there is precipitation on a planet with an amount of carbon dioxide in its atmosphere higher than Earth's, perhaps the partial pressure of this gas can affect the amount of water vapor that leaves the liquid phase and enters the gaseous phase.

Remember that one gram of pure liquid water absorbs 540 calories during the phase change from liquid to water vapor. This is known as the boiling point.

Boiling of a liquid does not necessarily mean a liquid must be hot. Certain liquids can boil well below water's boiling point temperature: rubbing alcohol and methyl chloride (found in Christmas ornaments called "bubblers") are two such liquids.

The lamp used in this experiment is simulating a noon-day summer sun in Southern California.

PURPOSE

The purpose of this experiment is to create a carbon dioxide/nitrogen atmosphere. This model will attempt to influence the amount of moisture evaporated from actual land form samples.

MATERIALS NEEDED

- aquarium
- glass cover
- 1 ring stand with clamp
- 1 100-watt white lamp
- 1 lamp shield
- 6 metal heating screens

- goggles
- 1 candle and candle holder
- triple beam balance
- 10-ml graduated cylinder
- 3 shallow pans or evaporating dishes
- samples of: sand, dirt, grass blades (fresh)
- masking tape
- 100 ml tap water

PROCEDURE

Caution! The metal heating screens, lamp, and shield will become hot.

1. See FIG. 14-1 for experiment setup.
2. Label 3 strips of masking tape: sand, dirt, and grass. Tape each to a dish or pan.
3. See FIG. 14-2 for the data table. Make copies as needed for the other atmospheres.
4. Weigh the evaporating dishes (or pans) to the nearest 0.01 gram.
5. Record this value in FIG. 14-2.
6. Place a sample of sand, dirt, and grass blades into each pan.
7. Weigh each pan again to the nearest 0.01 gram. Record this value in FIG. 14-2.
8. Add (carefully measured with the graduated cylinder) 2.0 ml of water to each substance in its pan.
9. Weigh the pans again. Record the masses on FIG. 14-2. Perform the subtractions.
10. Place the pans inside the aquarium.
11. See "Experiment preparation techniques" on page xix for a carbon dioxide atmosphere.
12. Wear goggles when using any open flame.
13. Be sure at least 6 heating screens are used to prevent the candle's heat from cracking the glass cover.
14. After the candle flame is out, let the water which has condensed on the walls of the aquarium change back into water vapor. (This takes about 15 minutes.)
15. Be sure the lamp is at least 25 cm above the glass cover.
16. Turn the lamp on and start heating for at least 24 hours.
    After 24 hours
17. Turn the lamp off.
18. Carefully remove the masking tape from the glass cover.
19. Remove the cover from the aquarium.
20. Take each pan out of the tank.
21. Weigh all pans again.
22. Record these masses on FIG. 14-2.
23. Subtract the mass of the pan for each substance to determine mass of water evaporated.

24. See FIG. 14-3 for previously recorded data for a carbon dioxide atmosphere.

25. Figures 14-4 and 14-5 are previously recorded data for a sealed "air atmosphere" and an "open air atmosphere."

26. If this lab is being performed for a sealed "air atmosphere" and an "open air atmosphere," be sure to use the same masses of all substances each time. Repeat the previous steps.

27. Discard all used materials in the appropriate waste containers.

OBSERVATIONS

Compare the amounts of water evaporated from the substances in each atmosphere. Which had the greatest evaporation? Why is this?

QUESTIONS

Did it seem that the carbon dioxide atmosphere allowed more evaporation than the sealed air atmosphere? Why is this?

Why was the greatest amount of evaporation from the unsealed aquarium? Would this amount vary if the experiment were performed on a rainy day as opposed to a hot, sunny day? Why?

EARTH EVENT

Perform this experiment again, but use twice as much of each substance. Keep the amount of water added the same. Does the amount of substance affect how much or how little water is evaporated?

Try other colored lamps (red, green, or blue 100-watt). How does a different light color affect evaporation?

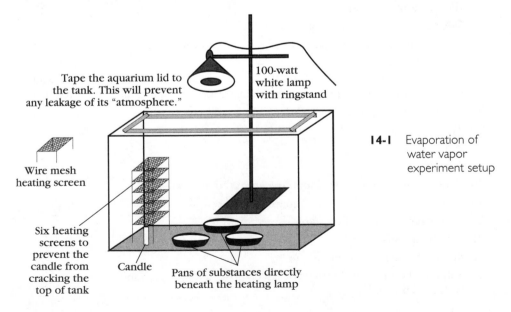

Tape the aquarium lid to the tank. This will prevent any leakage of its "atmosphere."

100-watt white lamp with ringstand

Wire mesh heating screen

Six heating screens to prevent the candle from cracking the top of tank

Candle

Pans of substances directly beneath the heating lamp

14-1 Evaporation of water vapor experiment setup

14-2 Evaporation of water vapor data table

		Substance		
		Dirt	Sand	Grass
Mass of dish (grams)	A			
Mass of dish with substance (grams)	B			
Mass of "dry" substance (grams)	(B−A)			
Add 2 ml water				
Mass of dish with substance and water (grams)	C			
Mass of "wetted" substance (grams)	(C−A)			
Begin heating . . .				
Mass of dish and substance after 24 hours (grams)	D			
Mass of water evaporated (grams)	(C−D)			

14-3 Evaporation of water vapor sample data table (CO_2 atmosphere, sealed aquarium)

		Substance		
		Dirt	Sand	Grass
Mass of dish (grams)	A	72.90	72.50	72.40
Mass of dish with substance (grams)	B	106.25	109.90	76.75
Mass of "dry" substance (grams)	(B−A)	33.35	37.40	4.35
Add 2 ml water				
Mass of dish with substance and water (grams)	C	108.25	111.90	78.75
Mass of "wetted" substance (grams)	(C−A)	35.35	39.40	6.35
Begin heating . . .				
Mass of dish and substance after 24 hours (grams)	D	105.90	109.90	73.35
Mass of water evaporated (grams)	(C−D)	2.35	2.00	5.40

		Substance		
		Dirt	Sand	Grass
Mass of dish (grams)	A	72.90	72.50	72.40
Mass of dish with substance (grams)	B	106.25	109.90	76.75
Mass of "dry" substance (grams)	(B−A)	33.35	37.40	4.35
Add 2 ml water				
Mass of dish with substance and water (grams)	C	108.25	111.90	78.75
Mass of "wetted" substance (grams)	(C−A)	35.35	39.40	6.35
Begin heating . . .				
Mass of dish and substance after 24 hours (grams)	D	106.00	110.00	73.35
Mass of water evaporated (grams)	(C−D)	2.25	1.90	5.00

14-4 Evaporation of water vapor sample data table (N_2/O_2 atmosphere, sealed aquarium)

		Substance		
		Dirt	Sand	Grass
Mass of dish (grams)	A	72.90	72.50	72.40
Mass of dish with substance (grams)	B	106.25	109.90	76.75
Mass of "dry" substance (grams)	(B−A)	33.25	37.40	4.35
Add 2 ml water				
Mass of dish with substance and water (grams)	C	108.25	111.90	78.75
Mass of "wetted" substance (grams)	(C−A)	35.35	39.40	6.35
Begin heating . . .				
Mass of dish and substance after 24 hours (grams)	D	105.60	109.90	73.55
Mass of water evaporated (grams)	(C−D)	2.65	2.05	5.50

14-5 Evaporation of water vapor sample data table (N_2/O_2 atmosphere, exposed to classroom air)

The following facts have been paraphrased from a variety of sources (nearly 400): TV, magazines, research papers, newspapers, and reference books:

- Bacteria that do not require oxygen to live may not only be limited to staying as simple creatures on Earth, but in an atmosphere such as Jupiter's, they (and not the oxygen-breathing forms) might be the start of the evolutionary mainstream.

- Some small organisms on Earth can survive under a wide range of pressures: certain fungus can withstand 3000 times normal Earth pressure. (Standard pressure on Earth at sea-level is 14.7 pounds psi or 760 mm Hg.)

- Natural selection (on any planet) will most likely lead to the dominant forms of life that are best suited to the common (or average) weather conditions on that planet.

- Different types of organisms on different planets will perform different functions: a small creature will eat most of the time to keep generating heat, while a large creature will be concerned with how to rid its body of excess heat. This is not unlike life on Earth. Plants at low temperatures on Earth absorb more infrared rays from the sun than do plants at moderate temperatures. In very cold climates, this increased infrared absorption would make a plant look more "blue" in color when sunlight strikes it.

- At very high temperatures, plants would reflect more infrared radiation (and that part of the spectrum). Such plants would appear more "red" in color when sunlight strikes it.

- Some algae in springs near the boiling point of water tend to be bright orange in color.

- Life's temperatures:
  Venus Life on this type of planet would be concerned with eliminating excess heat to stay cooler than the surroundings.
  Mars Life on this type of planet would try to store heat energy to stay warmer in frigid temperatures.
  Earth The temperature of "life" on Earth is nearly the same as the temperature of the planet's surface itself.

☆ ☆ ☆ ☆ ☆ ☆ ☆ ☆ ☆ ☆ ☆ ☆ ☆ ☆ ☆ ☆ ☆ ☆ ☆ ☆

Evaporation of water vapor from land with a CO_2/N_2 atmosphere

15
Heating/cooling of land with a CO$_2$/N$_2$ atmosphere

In an atmosphere composed mostly of carbon dioxide, will this gas affect the heating of the landscape? Will it help to heat the land/water faster? Or will it behave as an insulating "blanket" keeping out this heat?

Mars is a planet with a mostly carbon dioxide atmosphere. Its atmosphere contains no oxygen. It is also further from the Sun than the Earth. It is quite a dry planet. (Umbrellas will not be needed when visiting there!)

Different atmospheric gases absorb and reflect solar radiation at different wavelengths. Measuring the amount of absorption and which wavelengths of radiation are absorbed (by these gases) will tell astronomers what amount of gases compose the planet's atmosphere.

PURPOSE

The purpose of this experiment is to construct a carbon dioxide/nitrogen atmosphere. This model will attempt to influence the heating and cooling temperatures of actual land forms.

MATERIALS NEEDED

- aquarium
- glass cover
- masking tape
- 6 metal heating screens
- test tube rack
- 5 test tubes
- 5 alcohol thermometers
- goggles
- 1 candle
- 1 candle holder
- clock or watch with second hand

- samples of: dry sand and dirt, grass blades (fresh), tap water, and salt water (3.5% NaCl)

If performed indoors

- 1 100-watt white lamp
- 1 lamp shield
- 1 ring stand with clamp

PROCEDURE

Caution! The metal heating screens, lamp, and shield will become hot.

1. See FIG. 15-1 for experiment setup.
2. See "Experiment preparation techniques" on page xix to set up for a carbon dioxide atmosphere and on page xx to make a 3.5% salt solution.
3. Fill five test tubes approximately ¾ with: sand, dirt, grass, tap and salt (3.5% NaCl) water.
4. Place a thermometer in each test tube.
5. Do not use a rubber stopper. (The carbon dioxide atmosphere must reach the substance in each test tube.)
6. Place the test tubes in a test tube rack.
7. Place the rack in the aquarium.
8. Wear goggles when using any open flame.
9. Light the candle in the tank.
10. Cover the tank with the glass cover.
11. Tape the cover to the aquarium with masking tape.
12. If the lab is performed outdoors, place the aquarium outside on a wood table in direct sunlight between the hours of 10 a.m. and 2 p.m. If performed indoors, place the lamp 25 cm away from the glass cover.
13. Record beginning temperatures on FIG. 15-2.
14. As the oxygen is slowly being exhausted, record the heating temperatures at the 5 and 10 minute marks.
15. The candle flame will extinguish after approximately 9 minutes. (This depends on the size of the aquarium.)
16. If performed outdoors, bring the aquarium back into the classroom after 10 minutes. If performed indoors, turn the lamp off after 10 minutes to allow cooling.
17. Record cooling temperatures at the 15 and 20 minute marks.
18. Clean out the aquarium and let the thermometers return to room temperature.
19. If the tank is to be used again, use new samples of substances.
20. Repeat these procedures.
21. See FIGS. 15-3 and 15-4 for previously recorded data in the carbon dioxide and nitrogen atmospheres respectively.
22. Discard used materials in the appropriate waste containers.

OBSERVATIONS

From the example data tables (FIGS. 15-3 and 15-4), the substances heated slightly higher and cooled slightly lower in the carbon dioxide atmosphere than in the sealed "air" atmosphere. How does your data compare to these data tables?

Does such an atmosphere influence the temperatures?

QUESTIONS

How does excess carbon dioxide contribute to excessive heating on the planet Venus?

As more carbon dioxide is generated here on Earth, how will this affect global temperatures?

EARTH EVENT

Perform the experiment again, but do not seal the aquarium. (The sealed aquarium behaves as a small greenhouse.) Having the substances heat in the open will produce different heating temperatures.

Graph your results on separate sheets of graph paper. Be sure to use the appropriate scale to fit all recorded temperatures. Your graph will have five lines. How do the slopes of the temperatures of the materials in the carbon dioxide atmosphere compare with the temperatures in the air?

For best results, perform this experiment outside on a sunny day between the hours of 11 am to 2 pm.

If this experiment is performed inside the laboratory, use a 100-watt clear lamp. The lamp should be at least 25 cm above the top center of the aquarium.

15-1 Heating/cooling with CO_2 experiment setup

Substance	Heating/cooling temperatures every 5 minutes (°C)					
	0		5	10		15	20
Sand							
Dirt		Heating			Cooling		
Grass							
Tap water							
Salt water							

15-2 Heating/cooling with CO_2 data table

Substance	Heating/cooling temperatures every 5 minutes (°C)						
	0		5	10		15	20
Sand	25		29	32.5		33.5	32.5
Dirt	24	Heating	29.5	34	Cooling	33.5	32
Grass	24		31	36		34	32.5
Tap water	23		26.5	29		29	29
Salt water	23		27	29.5		29.5	29.5

15-3 Heating/cooling sample data table (N_2/CO_2)

Substance	Heating/cooling temperatures every 5 minutes (°C)						
	0		5	10		15	20
Sand	24		27	31.5		32	32
Dirt	24	Heating	29	33.5	Cooling	34	32
Grass	25		29	34.5		35	33.5
Tap water	23		26	28.5		29	29.5
Salt water	23.5		26.5	29		30	30

15-4 Heating/cooling example data table (N_2/O_2)

Heating/cooling of land with a CO_2/N_2 atmosphere **71**

16
Evaporation rates of different salinity waters in a CO$_2$/N$_2$ atmosphere

Since Mars has an atmosphere made mostly of carbon dioxide (argon and nitrogen are also present) how would this atmosphere affect the evaporation of any oceans that might exist?

First, it must be said that the amount of precipitable water of the Martian atmosphere is 0.001 inch. This means that if all the water in Mars' atmosphere suddenly condensed out of its sky, it would cover the planet with water to a depth of 0.001 inch.

Earth has one thousand times the amount of precipitable water. Also, it has a fraction of carbon dioxide in its atmosphere.

In this experiment, the salinity of model oceans will be varied. Compared to the average 3.5% surface salinity of Earth's oceans, a salinity of a 7.0% and 10.5% model ocean will be made to evaporate in a mostly carbon dioxide atmosphere.

Will the partial pressure of a large amount of CO$_2$ gas affect the evaporation of an ocean? How will the different amounts of salt dissolved in each ocean affect the amounts of water evaporated from each?

PURPOSE

The purpose of this experiment is to construct a carbon dioxide/nitrogen atmosphere. This model will attempt to influence the evaporation of samples of ocean water at different salinities: normal salinity, twice normal salinity, and three times normal salinity.

MATERIALS NEEDED

- aquarium
- glass cover
- masking tape
- 6 metal heating screens

- 1 candle
- 1 candle holder
- 5 evaporating dishes or shallow pans
- 1 alcohol thermometer
- 100-watt white lamp
- 1 lamp shield
- 1 ring stand with clamp
- samples of: distilled water, tap water, salt water: 3.5%, 7.0%, and 10.5% NaCl
- clock
- goggles
- centimeter ruler

PROCEDURE

Caution! The metal heating screens, lamp, and shield will become hot.

1. See FIG. 16-1 for experiment setup.
2. Make the appropriate number of copies of FIG. 16-2 to record data for the different atmospheres.
3. First, experiment with the carbon dioxide atmosphere. Refer to "Experiment Preparation Techniques" on pages xix and xx to set up for the carbon dioxide atmosphere and to prepare the correct salinity of the salt water samples.
4. Fill all pans with a sample of water to a level of 2.0 cm on a level surface.
5. Place all pans in the tank.
6. Wear goggles when using any open flame.
7. Light the candle inside the tank.
8. Place the heating screens over the candle.
9. Cover the aquarium with the glass cover.
10. Seal the tank with masking tape strips.
11. Be sure the light is 25 cm away from the top of the tank.
12. Turn the lamp on to begin heating.
13. After 20 minutes, record the beginning temperature on FIG. 16-2.
14. Heat the tank's substances for 24 hours.
    After 24 hours
15. Large drops of water should be on the upper glass cover opposite from the light.
16. Record the ending temperature on FIG. 16-2.
17. Remove the masking tape from the glass cover.
18. Take the glass cover off the aquarium.
19. Carefully remove each pan.
20. Place all pans on a level surface.
21. Measure the level of water in each pan. Be sure to dry the ruler on a towel after each use.

22. Record the new levels on FIG. 16-2.

23. Calculate the amount of water evaporated for each substance.

24. See FIG. 16-3 for previously recorded data for the carbon dioxide atmosphere.

25. Pour out the water from the aquarium.

26. Dry the aquarium thoroughly for the next atmosphere.

27. Repeat the experiment using these procedures, but do not prepare a carbon dioxide atmosphere. (The screens and candle are not needed for the other atmospheres, only the thermometer.)

28. See FIGS. 16-4 and 16-5 for data recorded for "air" atmospheres.

OBSERVATIONS

Which sample of water had the greatest amount of evaporation in the air atmosphere? How did the carbon dioxide affect the evaporation of each sample?

QUESTIONS

Why did the most evaporation occur from the unsealed aquarium?

EARTH EVENT

Where on the planet Earth does the most evaporation take place? Does it occur in an area of great rainfall? Where would the least amount of evaporation occur? Would it occur in a desert area? Explain.

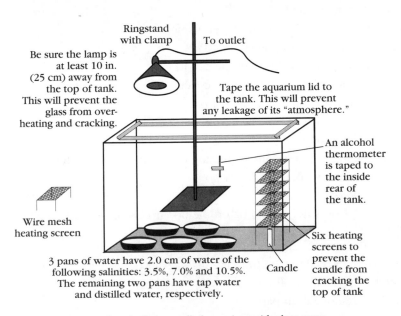

Ringstand with clamp   To outlet

Be sure the lamp is at least 10 in. (25 cm) away from the top of tank. This will prevent the glass from over-heating and cracking.

Tape the aquarium lid to the tank. This will prevent any leakage of its "atmosphere."

An alcohol thermometer is taped to the inside rear of the tank.

Wire mesh heating screen

3 pans of water have 2.0 cm of water of the following salinities: 3.5%, 7.0% and 10.5%. The remaining two pans have tap water and distilled water, respectively.

Candle

Six heating screens to prevent the candle from cracking the top of tank

Standard glass-walled aquarium with glass cover

16-1   Evaporation rates experiment setup (CO_2/N_2)

Substance	A Initial height (cm)	B Final height (cm)	A−B Difference (cm)
Distilled			
Tap			
3.5%			
7.0%			
10.5%			

Starting temperature (°C) [ ]

Ending temperature (°C) [ ]

Atmosphere used: N_2/CO_2 N_2/O_2 N_2/O_2 (unsealed, exposed to classroom air)

16-2 Evaporation rates data table

Substance	A Initial height (cm)	B Final height (cm)	A−B Difference (cm)
Distilled	2.0	0.7	1.3
Tap	2.0	1.6	0.4
3.5%	2.0	1.5	0.5
7.0%	2.0	1.3	0.7
10.5%	2.0	1.2	0.8

Starting temperature (°C) [30]

Ending temperature (°C) [33]

Atmosphere used: (N_2/CO_2) N_2/O_2 N_2/O_2 (unsealed, exposed to classroom air)

16-3 Evaporation rates sample data table (CO_2/N_2)

Evaporation rates of different salinity waters in a CO_2/N_2 atmosphere **75**

Substance	A Initial height (cm)	B Final height (cm)	A−B Difference (cm)
Distilled	2.0	1.5	0.5
Tap	2.0	1.2	0.8
3.5%	2.0	1.2	0.8
7.0%	2.0	1.8	0.2
10.5%	2.0	1.9	0.1

Starting temperature (°C)	27
Ending temperature (°C)	29
Atmosphere used: N_2/CO_2 ⟨N_2/O_2⟩ N_2/O_2 (unsealed, exposed to classroom air)	

16-4 Evaporation rates sample data table (N_2/O_2)

Substance	A Initial height (cm)	B Final height (cm)	A−B Difference (cm)
Distilled	2.0	1.4	0.6
Tap	2.0	1.0	1.0
3.5%	2.0	1.5	0.5
7.0%	2.0	1.5	0.5
10.5%	2.0	1.5	0.5

Starting temperature (°C)	29
Ending temperature (°C)	30.5
Atmosphere used: N_2/CO_2 N_2/O_2 ⟨N_2/O_2 (unsealed, exposed to classroom air)⟩	

16-5 Evaporation rates sample data table (N_2/O_2, unsealed aquarium)

17
Decay rates of plant matter in a CO$_2$/N$_2$ atmosphere

The diatomic molecule oxygen is needed to permit combustion of food in the body, the rusting of iron, and the decay of plant matter. How would organic matter decay in an atmosphere composed of carbon dioxide? Would it retard spoilage?

Mars has a carbon dioxide atmosphere with other gases present: argon, nitrogen, and a trace of water vapor. There are probably thousands of planets (throughout our Galaxy) where life-sustaining oxygen (as Earth possesses it) is only a tiny fraction of the atmosphere.

Perhaps the Martian atmosphere would be an excellent food dehydrator! With the cold temperatures and low oxygen content, such an atmosphere would not be capable of supporting life as we know it.

Yet, there are regions on Mars that are green during the Martian spring and turn brown over time. Is this vegetation during a seasonal change? Certainly another exploration of Mars is needed. Humans should explore the next time.

PURPOSE

The purpose of this experiment is to construct a carbon dioxide/nitrogen atmosphere. This model will attempt to influence the subsequent oxidation of an apple.

MATERIALS NEEDED

- aquarium
- glass cover
- masking tape
- 2 apples
- knife
- 6 heating screens
- 1 candle
- 1 candle holder

- goggles
- 1 100-ml beaker
- 1 alcohol thermometer

PROCEDURE

Caution! The metal heating screens, lamp, and shield will become hot. Handle the sharp cutting knife with care or under adult supervision.

1. See FIG. 17-1 for experiment setup.
2. Refer to "Experiment Preparation Techniques" on page xix to prepare the aquarium for its "atmosphere."
3. Tape an alcohol thermometer to the inside back wall of the tank with masking tape.
4. Place at least 6 metal wire heating screens in one corner of the aquarium.
5. Wear goggles when using any open flame.
6. Using a candle and candle holder, light the candle and place it under the heating screens.
7. Cut an apple in half.
8. Place one apple half in the aquarium resting on a clean and dry 100 ml glass beaker.
9. Cover the aquarium with the glass cover.
10. Seal the aquarium completely with masking tape strips.
11. Place the aquarium outside on a wooden table.
12. Under this wooden table, tape a thermometer. This thermometer will measure the outside air temperature.
13. Place the other apple half outside in sunlight resting in its own 100-ml beaker.
14. Record beginning oxidation amounts to both apple halves on FIG. 17-2.
15. At the 10 and 30 minute marks, evaluate the amount of oxidation to both apple halves.
16. Record these values on FIG. 17-2.
17. After 30 minutes, record the temperatures of both thermometers on FIG. 17-2.
18. Discard the used apple halves.
19. If another aquarium is available, perform the experiment again, but do not make a carbon dioxide atmosphere.
20. Place the aquarium outside.
21. Keep the other apple half inside the classroom.
22. See FIG. 17-3 for previously recorded data.
23. Discard the used materials in the appropriate waste containers.

OBSERVATIONS

Which portion of the experiment had the greatest amount of oxidation to the apple half?

What role does carbon dioxide play in the oxidation of the apple half?

QUESTIONS

Would a piece of fruit rot on the surface of Mars? Explain.

EARTH EVENT

If an apple is not available, substitute another material. Bartlett pears work quite nicely when the exposed half is used.

Suggestion: Try a sliced raw potato half.

Tank preparation for the formation of carbon dioxide "atmosphere"

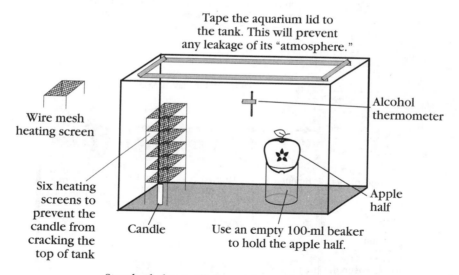

Tape the aquarium lid to the tank. This will prevent any leakage of its "atmosphere."

Alcohol thermometer

Wire mesh heating screen

Six heating screens to prevent the candle from cracking the top of tank

Candle

Use an empty 100-ml beaker to hold the apple half.

Apple half

Standard glass-walled aquarium with glass cover

17-1 Decay rates experiment setup

Oxidation scale legend

| | 1 | 2 | 3 | 4 | 5 |

Atmosphere used	Beginning oxidation	After 10 minutes	After 30 minutes	Temperature after 30 minutes (°C)
N₂/O₂ sealed aquarium (sunlight)	1 2 3 4 5	1 2 3 4 5	1 2 3 4 5	
N₂/O₂ (not covered) inside classroom	1 2 3 4 5	1 2 3 4 5	1 2 3 4 5	
N₂/O₂ (not covered) outside sunlight	1 2 3 4 5	1 2 3 4 5	1 2 3 4 5	
N₂/CO₂ sealed aquarium (sunlight)	1 2 3 4 5	1 2 3 4 5	1 2 3 4 5	

Note: This is (CO₂)

Circle the number that indicates the amount of oxidation to the apple half. A (1) indicates no oxidation. A (5) indicates complete oxidation (i.e., the apple half is completely brown).

17-2 Decay rates data table

This data was recorded on a sunny July day at 1 pm, local time

Oxidation scale legend

| | 1 | 2 | 3 | 4 | 5 |

Atmosphere used	Beginning oxidation	After 10 minutes	After 30 minutes	Temperature after 30 minutes (°C)
N₂/O₂ sealed aquarium (sunlight)	①2 3 4 5	1②3 4 5	1 2③4 5	46
N₂/O₂ (not covered) inside classroom	①2 3 4 5	1 2③4 5	1 2 3④5	24
N₂/O₂ (not covered) outside sunlight	①2 3 4 5	1②3 4 5	1 2 3④5	32
N₂/CO₂ sealed aquarium (sunlight)	①2 3 4 5	1②3 4 5	1②3 4 5	37

Note: This is (CO₂)

Circle the number that indicates the amount of oxidation to the apple half. A (1) indicates no oxidation. A (5) indicates complete oxidation (i.e., the apple half is completely brown).

17-3 Decay rates sample data table

Geophysical Features

Earth is blessed with a variety of features: mountain barriers, oceans, lakes, continents, and valleys. What the weather will be like tomorrow is influenced greatly by these landforms.

Imagine for a moment the existence of oceans where pure water ice sinks, different colored suns heat the landscape, smoke filled atmospheres inhibit the heating and cooling effects of solar radiation, icebergs melt in higher salinity oceans, and red and blue suns cast their own shadows.

What would the weather be like on such planets?

All differences in barometric pressure between places on the surface of the Earth result from being directly or indirectly influenced by temperature differences. Warm air rises and low pressure results; cool air sinks and raises barometric pressure.

When surface areas are compared, our planet has a water to land ratio of 7 to 3. On a planet with a higher ratio of water to land (8 to 2 or 9 to 1) all land would be completely surrounded by oceans everywhere.

Such planets would have very different pressure, temperature and humidity patterns.

On a planet with very little water (Mars' landscape is an example) dust storms would rake the ground.

Earth has just the right proportions. Along with the season-forming tilt of 23.5° to Earth's axis, they cause uneven heating and cooling of the geophysical features.

These ingredients provide a most interesting array of weather events for all Earth's inhabitants.

18

Melting rates of non-floating ice

If water did not have the property of expanding during its phase change of liquid to solid, it would sink. Sunken ice would never melt. Probably all rivers and oceans would have stayed frozen solid after the Earth became more geologically stable.

It is this feature of ice that allows life to exist under such a frozen "skin" in rivers and lakes.

There could be planets with liquid oceans of different densities. With a liquid less dense than that of pure water (1.00 g/ml), H_2O ice would sink.

If this ice sank during a planet's winter in shallow ponds or lakes, quite possibly rays from a sun during the spring and summer seasons would penetrate these depths enough to melt the ice.

Underwater creep (by the more dense H_2O) might occur. The water could eventually migrate to an area where evaporation could take place and it would enter again this planet's hydrologic cycle.

This experiment is a model to show how at what rate H_2O ice melts while completely submerged.

PURPOSE

The purpose of this experiment is to observe how a liquid less dense than [H_2O] ice causes the ice to sink. Here, the ice will gradually warm and melt.

MATERIALS NEEDED

- 1 500-ml beaker
- 400 ml of isopropyl or methyl alcohol (burner fuel)
- ice cube
- 1 alcohol thermometer
- clock or watch with second hand
- goggles

PROCEDURE

Caution! Avoid breathing the vapors of the isopropyl or methyl alcohol. Wear goggles while pouring either of these liquids.

1. See FIG. 18-1 for experiment setup.
2. Pour at least 400 ml of isopropyl or methyl alcohol (burner fuel) into a 500-ml glass beaker.
3. Place the beaker on a wood table or desk.
4. Place an alcohol thermometer in the beaker.
5. Record a beginning temperature on FIG. 18-2.
6. Gently, drop an ice cube into the beaker.
7. Record temperatures every minute on FIG. 18-2.
8. At the 5 and 10 minute mark, stir the solution for 2 seconds.
9. Record the time the ice cube melts completely on FIG. 18-2.
10. Continue recording temperatures of the alcohol solution until it stabilizes (approximately 3 more minutes).
11. After the experiment, pour the alcohol down the drain with plenty of water.
12. See FIG. 18-3 for previously recorded data.

OBSERVATIONS

Why was the solution stirred at minutes 5 and 10?
    At what time did the ice cube melt in the beaker?

QUESTIONS

If liquid water and another liquid less dense than water existed on a planet, how might this affect the freezing of lakes or rivers? (Assume that the less dense liquid has a lower freezing point than water.)

EARTH EVENT

Perform this experiment again, but use room temperature tap water to melt the ice cube. Stir at 5 and 10 minutes. When does the ice cube melt?

Graph your results on a sheet of graph paper. How do the slopes of the temperatures of the melting submerged ice compare to those of the ice melting in water?

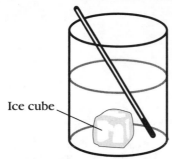

Alcohol thermometer

500 ml beaker with 400 ml of isopropyl (or methyl) alcohol.

Begin timing when the ice cube reaches the bottom of the beaker.

Ice cube

Stir for two seconds at the 5- and 10-minute mark. Continue timing to the 15-minute mark, if needed.

Perform this experiment on a wood table or desk. This will prevent any heat from affecting the melting of the ice cube at the bottom of this beaker.

18-1   Melting rates of non-floating ice experiment setup

Time (minutes)	Temperature (°/C)
0	
1	
2	
3	
4	
5	
6	
7	
8	
9	
10	
11	
12	
13	
14	
15	

Circle the time at which the ice cube finally melts.

Ice cube melted at:
_____ min. _____ sec.

18-2   Melting rates of non-floating ice data table

Time (minutes)	Temperature (°/C)
0	23
1	17
2	13
3	11.5
4	11
5	11
6	14
7	13
8	12
9	12
10	13
(11)	16
12	17
13	17
14	17
15	17

Circle the time at which the
ice cube finally melts.

Ice cube melted at:
__11__ min. __22__ sec.

18-3   Melting rates of non-floating ice example data table

☆ ☆ **FACTOIDS** ☆ ☆

The following facts have been paraphrased from a
variety of sources (nearly 400): TV, magazines, research
papers, newspapers, and reference books:

- Three "revolutions" have occurred in the history of
humans.

    The first was the notion that we are not the center
    of the solar system but that our Earth revolves
    about the sun with other planets.

    The second was the discovery that humankind is
    not outside the animal kingdom but is actually a
    part of it.

    The third was the notion that our galaxy is not the
    center of the universe but that we are a part of a
    larger system of space.

    The fourth would be the revelation that a planet
    outside our Solar System has been discovered.

    The fifth would be to find new life on this planet (or
    somewhere else) and would be the most humbling
    revolution of all. Perhaps it would be the most
    frightening. We should welcome these life forms, not
    as enemies, but perhaps not as friends, either.

19
Melting rates of icebergs in oceans of different salinities

Icebergs floating in the Atlantic off the East Coast are quite a menace to shipping. They melt at a fixed rate in the salty oceans and cannot be made to melt faster by human intervention.

But how would different salinity levels affect the melting rates? The salinity of ocean water varies. It averages 3.5% at the surface and raises to much higher levels at further depths.

Would a higher salt content assist in fracturing the ice crystal faster than a normal salinity ocean?

Perhaps there exist liquid oceans on other planets of higher salinities. The extra amount of dissolved solids may be a factor in the melting rate of pure H_2O ice.

PURPOSE

The purpose of this experiment is to observe how different salinity "oceans" (normal salinity, twice normal salinity, and three times normal salinity) affects the melting rate of H_2O ice.

MATERIALS NEEDED

- 5 500-ml beakers
- 5 alcohol thermometers
- masking tape
- ice cubes
- samples of: distilled water, tap water, salt water (3.5, 7.0, and 10.5% NaCl)
- clock or watch with second hand

PROCEDURE

Caution! Although not normally poisonous, powdered sodium chloride (NaCl) can be an irritant to eyes or mouth. Wash with plenty of cold water if some should get on skin or face.

1. See FIG. 19-1 for experiment setup.
2. See "Experiment Preparation Techniques" on page xx to make a 3.5, 7.0, and 10.5% NaCl water solution. These solutions will not be heated.
3. Use 5 500-ml glass beakers.
4. Place a strip of masking tape on the outside of each beaker.
5. Label each beaker with the appropriate solution used.
6. Pour 400 ml of each solution into each beaker.
7. Place a thermometer in each beaker.
8. Place all beakers on a wood table or desk.
9. Do not use a heating lamp.
10. Record all beginning temperatures on FIG. 19-2.
11. Place an ice cube into each beaker.
12. Record temperatures each minute on FIG. 19-2.
13. *Do not stir* the solutions.
14. Record the time when each ice cube melts at the bottom of FIG. 19-2.
15. After the experiment, pour all solutions down the drain. Rinse with cold water.
16. See FIG. 19-3 for a table of previously recorded data.

OBSERVATIONS

In which solution did the ice cube melt first? Explain.

Refer to FIG. 19-3. Ignore the distilled and tap water times. Why did the ice melt first in the 10.5% NaCl solution? (This experiment was performed four times, to confirm these readings.) How do your values compare to the ones in FIG. 19-3?

QUESTIONS

How quickly might icebergs melt, floating in oceans with salinities greater than our own?

What possible reason could explain the greater levels of salinity of oceans on different planets? (Hint: Erosion from rain/snow fall brings sediments and minerals to the sea.)

EARTH EVENT

Perform this experiment again, but place the beakers out in direct sunlight. Which salt solution slows the melting of ice in such direct light?

The beakers are at room temperature only. Do not add heat or use any lights for heating.

| Distilled | Tap | 3.5% | 7.0% | 10.5% |

Perform this experiment on a wood table or desk. This will prevent any heat at the bottom of this beaker from affecting the melting of the ice cube.

19-1 Melting rates of icebergs experiment setup

Time (minutes)	Water temperature (°C)				
	Distilled	Tap	3.5%	7.0%	10.5%
0					
1					
2					
3					
4					
5					
6					
7					
8					
9					
10					

Time ice cube melted in each substance:

Distilled   Tap   3.5%
____ min. ____ sec.   ____ min. ____ sec.   ____ min. ____ sec.

                7.0%   10.5%
        ____ min. ____ sec.   ____ min. ____ sec.

19-2 Melting rates of icebergs data table

Time (minutes)	Water temperature (°C)				
	Distilled	Tap	3.5%	7.0%	10.5%
0	22	22	22	22	22
1	22	19	20	19	19
2	21	17	20	18.5	18
3	21	17.5	18	18	18
4	21	17	17	17	17
5	21	17	17	17	17
6	21	17	17	16.5	17
7	21	17	17	17	17
8	21	17	17.5	17	17
9	21	17	17.5	17	17
10	21	17	17.5	17	17.5

Time ice cube melted in each substance:

Distilled
_5_ min. _15_ sec.

Tap
_5_ min. _35_ sec.

3.5%
_10_ min. _22_ sec.

7.0%
_9_ min. _14_ sec.

10.5%
_8_ min. _20_ sec.

19-3 Melting rates of icebergs sample data table

☆ ☆ FACTOIDS ☆ ☆

The following facts have been paraphrased from a variety of sources (nearly 400): TV, magazines, research papers, newspapers, and reference books:

- Some simple bacteria on Earth can live in hot springs where the temperature is as high as 170° Fahrenheit.

- Some scientists believe that most of the chloride ions in surface rivers and streams in the world came from sodium chloride (table salt) washed out of the skies by rain. This salt came from the oceans as a tiny crystal blown by wind.

20

Temperatures of anti-red/anti-blue shadows from a binary star system

In exploring various planets in a nearby galaxy, you might encounter a double sun system. It might have a large red giant that is very old and a small, hot blue dwarf that is very young. Age here is spoken of in relation to cosmic time.

These two suns cast two colors of light on nearby planets: red light and blue light. Compare this to our sun casting its glow upon Earth.

Objects would cast two shadows. That is, the shadow is "filled in" with the light from the other sun, which is not blocked by the object. This is called the "Flammarion Effect" after the French astronomer who described it in 1894.

If one of the planets being explored had an atmosphere that could sustain life as we know it, the temperatures would be unlike those that we experience here on Earth.

If vegetation is overly sensitive to blue light and its growth favors red light, where might it "hide" on this planet? Would it be mobile enough to hide in one of the shadows cast by these suns?

Should this plant life be capable of living only in the cooler, red light, and hide from the warmer, blue light when that particular sun is visible? Could the opposite be true?

What would the temperatures of the surrounding terrain be like?

This laboratory exercise is a model of simple heating, but with a twist. The temperatures of the shadows cast from an object are measured and compared to shadow temperatures here on Earth.

PURPOSE

The purpose of this experiment is to observe the heating temperatures of differently colored shadows cast from a model binary sun system: red giant and blue dwarf.

MATERIALS NEEDED

- 1 white poster board
- 7 alcohol thermometers
- masking tape
- 2 lamps: 100-watt red, 100-watt blue
- 2 lamp shields
- wood block (3 cm × 3 cm × 20 cm)
- clock or watch with second hand

PROCEDURE

1. See FIG. 20-1 for experiment setup.
2. Briefly, turn lamps on to verify that the thermometers are within the shadows being cast by the wood block.
3. Thermometers 1 and 2 should be at least 4 cm away from each light's hood.
4. Let all temperatures on the thermometers come to room temperature.
5. Record these beginning temperatures on FIG. 20-2.
6. Turn lamps on to begin heating.
7. Record temperatures every minute for 10 minutes on FIG. 20-2.
8. At minute 10, turn lamps off. Let all materials cool to room temperature before putting equipment away. They can be quite warm.
9. See FIG. 20-3 for previously recorded data.

OBSERVATIONS

What direction was each shadow cast? Did you expect this? Why or why not?

Which shadow temperature was the coolest? the warmest?

Immediately behind the wood block is an area where no light reached. Why did this occur?

Why was the area between the colored shadows (the penumbra) so warm? Where does a penumbra occur when a tree on Earth casts a shadow?

QUESTIONS

Could these temperatures be potentially life-sustaining? What else would an organism require to live on a planet with suns similar to these?

How did your results compare to those in FIG. 20-3?

Vary the size of the object used and observe the shadow size. How would this change affect the area temperature?

EARTH EVENT

Try placing the white poster board outside in early morning or late afternoon sunlight (when shadows are longest). Measure the temperatures of the single shadow that is cast. Is it possible to measure any temperature differences?

Remember that thermal radiation takes place in straight lines. That is, heat cannot "bend" around objects (such as the Moon during a solar eclipse).

Back inside the laboratory, use two white lamps to cast two dark shadows. Try measuring the shadow temperatures. How do they compare to the anti-red and anti-blue temperatures?

Obviously, our simple "planet" had no rotation, hence the shadows did not change in length or position. Earth rotates one degree of longitude every four minutes. This causes a shift in shadow position and length. (Think of a sundial shadow!) How does this rotation affect any heating or cooling of Earth's surface?

Wood block used to cast shadow to
be measured by thermometers 3 and 4.
Wood is used because it is a poor conductor.

Blue lamp   Red lamp

To outlet

Tape each
thermometer
to the poster board
using masking
tape. Be sure the
readings are visible.

To outlet

(1)

(2)

(3)

Anti-blue
shadow

(4)

Anti-red
shadow

(5)

(6)

(7)

The area
immediately
behind the
block is where
no light falls.

The overlapping region of the two colored shadows is the
penumbra (a lighter region). Thermometer (#7) should be
located to the back of this region. On white poster board, the
shadows and colors are highly defined and easy to see.

20-1   Temperatures of anti-red/anti-blue shadows experiment setup

Heating time in minutes	Thermometer #/temperature (°C)						
	#1 (blue light)	#2 (red light)	#3 (anti-blue)	#5 (shadows)	#4 (anti-red)	#6 (shadows)	#7 (penumbra)
0							
1							
2							
3							
4							
5							
6							
7							
8							
9							
10							

20-2   Temperatures of anti-red/anti-blue shadows data table

Heating time in minutes	Thermometer #/temperature (°C)						
	#1 (blue light)	#2 (red light)	#3 (anti-blue)	#5 (shadows)	#4 (anti-red)	#6 (shadows)	#7 (penumbra)
0	27	27	28	28	28	28	28
1	29	29	31	29.5	29	28.5	31
2	29.5	29.5	31.5	30	29	29	32
3	30	30	32	30	29.5	29	32.5
4	31	30.5	32.5	30	30	29.5	33
5	31	31	33	30.5	30.5	30	33.5
6	32	32	33	30.5	31	30	34
7	32	32	33.5	31	31	30	34
8	32.5	32.5	34	31	31	30.5	34
9	33	33	34.5	31.5	31.5	30.5	34.5
10	33	33	34.5	31.5	32	31	35

20-3   Temperatures of anti-red/anti-blue shadows sample data table

21
Melting rate of ice in a smoke-filled atmosphere

In an atmosphere filled with smoke, would the temperatures be hotter or cooler than an atmosphere clear of smoke or haze?

Is it possible such a smoke layer could trap heat? Or would it reflect enough sunlight to keep the surface of a planet from heating excessively?

Is it possible that smoke-filled parts of Earth's atmosphere over certain cities in the world are actually negating the effects of the greenhouse effect? In other words, are we being kept cooler rather than warmer?

Here, the aquarium used will have a smoke source to completely fill the tank.

How quickly will an ice cube melt inside vs. outside the tank if placed out in the direct sunlight?

PURPOSE

The purpose of this experiment is to create an atmosphere filled with smoke particles. This model will attempt to influence the melting rate of ice placed inside the atmosphere.

MATERIALS NEEDED

- aquarium
- glass cover
- masking tape
- Five 500-ml beakers
- 7 alcohol thermometers
- ice cubes
- tap water
- newspaper strips
- goggles
- matches
- clock or watch with second hand

PROCEDURE

Caution! Avoid inhaling the smoke from the burning newspaper.

1. See FIG. 21-1 for experiment setup.
2. Fill beakers 1, 2, 3, and 4 with 300 ml of tap water.
3. Place thermometers into beakers 1 through 4.
4. Place beakers 3 and 4 into the aquarium.
5. Tape the two thermometers in the aquarium to the inside front glass securely with one masking tape strip.
6. Tape the thermometer (#7) under the table or hang it with string. (Thermometer #7 represents the outside temperature in the shade.)
7. Be sure the newspaper is torn into thin shreds. This will make burning easier and produce a thicker smoke more quickly.
8. Place at least 10 shredded pieces of paper in the beaker used for the smoke source.
9. Place a wooden table (desk or stand) outside the classroom on a sunny day. (Between the hours of 10 a.m. and 2 p.m. the rays of the sunlight are quite direct.)
10. Place one ice cube in beaker number 3 (see FIG. 21-1).
11. Place another ice cube in beaker number 1.
12. Wear goggles when using any open flame.
13. Light the paper in the beaker with a match.
14. Be sure enough paper in the beaker is burning to ensure a strong smoke source.
15. Place the beaker in the tank toward the back wall.
16. Seal the aquarium completely to retain the smoke generated.
17. Record all beginning temperatures on FIG. 21-2.
18. Record temperatures every 5 minutes.
19. When each ice cube melts, record the minute/second at the bottom of FIG. 21-2.
20. See FIG. 21-3 for a data table of previously recorded data.

OBSERVATIONS

How quickly did the ice cube in the smoke atmosphere melt compared to the outside cube?

Does the smoke layer promote or inhibit increases in temperature? Explain.

QUESTIONS

Forest fires, volcanic eruptions, even large meteorite crashes cause a tremendous amount of dust, smoke, and particles to fill the area above the catastrophe. How do these excessive amounts of particulates contribute to local weather?

Which disaster(s) above could affect weather globally? Explain.

EARTH EVENT

Graph your results and the results obtained in FIG. 21-3. Compare the two graphs. How does the slope for the ice inside the chamber compare to the ice outside?

How does time of day affect such heating or melting of the ice cube?

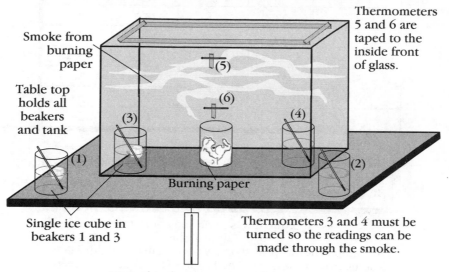

Standard glass-walled aquarium with glass cover

Tape the aquarium lid to the tank. This will prevent any leakage of smoke during the experiment.

Thermometers 5 and 6 are taped to the inside front of glass.

Smoke from burning paper

Table top holds all beakers and tank

(5)

(6)

(3)

(4)

(1)

(2)

Burning paper

Single ice cube in beakers 1 and 3

Thermometers 3 and 4 must be turned so the readings can be made through the smoke.

Hang this thermometer under the table with tape or string

21-1   Melting rate of ice in a smoke-filled atmosphere experiment setup

Thermometer #	Heating temperatures every 5 minutes (°C)			
	0	5	10	15
1				
2				
3				
4				
5				
6				
7				

In beaker number 1, the ice melted at: _____ min. _____ sec.

In beaker number 2, the ice melted at: _____ min. _____ sec.

21-2   Melting rate of ice data table

Thermometer #	Heating temperatures every 5 minutes (iC)			
	0	5	10	15
1	20	17.5	19	21
2	23	24.5	25.5	26
3	19	15.5	16.5	17.5
4	22	23	23	23.5
5	31	34	33	32
6	31	34	35	34
7	24	24	24	24

In beaker number 1, the ice melted at: __8__ min. __10__ sec.

In beaker number 2, the ice melted at: __9__ min. __33__ sec.

Note: This experiment was performed outside on a sunny day in July at 1 p.m.
All equipment was placed on a wooden table to reduce any heating from the ground. The height of the table was 4 feet.

☆ ☆ FACTOIDS ☆ ☆

The following facts have been paraphrased from a variety of sources (nearly 400): TV, magazines, research papers, newspapers, and reference books:

- Since no planets outside our solar system have been detected (yet), one method in use is to observe an object near a star giving off infrared radiation (as does our Earth). Such an object has not been found yet.

- Greenhouse gases (water vapor, carbon dioxide, methane, and nitrous oxide) are necessary on Earth to maintain the temperature of this planet. Of the four, humans are generating excess carbon dioxide at an unprecedented rate.

- Could virus molecules have been trapped within comets? The molecules could hypothetically fall upon the earth. Perhaps this could explain why certain viral diseases appear suddenly (ravaging animal/human populations) and then quickly die out.

22

Heating/cooling of actual land forms with a red, green, & blue sun

If it were possible to heat your electric stove top beyond that of a "red hot" burner, the color of the heating element would slowly change through the spectrum of visible light, from red to blue.

Temperatures would also change. A red element would be the coolest; blue would be the hottest.

Assume the planet being explored is orbiting one of these suns.

How would the surface (and water forms) heat under the intense rays of such a "noon-day" sun? Assume the suns are far enough away from the planet so as not to fry the land or evaporate the oceans.

PURPOSE

The purpose of this experiment is to observe the heating and cooling of actual land forms using model suns: red, green, and blue.

Materials needed

- 4 test tube racks with the following:
- 4 test tubes
- 4 alcohol thermometers
- 4 rubber stoppers (single hole)
- 4 100-watt lamps: red, green, blue, and white
- 4 lamp shields
- 4 ring stands with clamps
- samples of: dry sand and dirt, grass blades (fresh), tap water, and salt water (3.5% NaCl)
- clock or watch with second hand

PROCEDURE

1. See FIG. 22-1 for experiment setup. Although this figure only shows the setup for three lamps, use the white lamp (and its data) as a comparison for all other data recorded.

2. Fill 4 test tubes with samples of the following: dirt, sand, grass blades, tap water, and salt water

3. See " Experiment preparation techniques" on page xx to make a 3.5% salt solution.

4. Carefully, insert an alcohol thermometer into a one hole rubber stopper using soap water or glycerin.

5. Insert the stopper/thermometer assembly into the test tube. Be sure the bulb of the thermometer extends into the dirt and sand by at least 2 to 3 cm.

6. Place the 4 prepared test tubes into the front portion of a test tube rack.

7. Locate the four stations used around the classroom to minimize crowding by students.

8. Be sure each lamp is 25 cm away from the test tube rack.

9. Record beginning temperatures on FIGS. 22-2, 22-3, 22-4 for the red, green, and blue lamps.

10. Create a separate data table if the white lamp is used.

11. Turn on lamps to begin heating.

12. Record heating temperatures every minute until minute 10.

13. Turn off lamps at minute 10.

14. Record cooling temperatures until minute 20 on FIGS. 22-5, 22-6, and 22-7 for the red, green and blue lamps.

15. Make graphs similar to FIGS. 22-8 through 22-12. Be sure each graph represents only one substance.

16. Discard the used materials in the appropriate waste containers.

OBSERVATIONS

What substance under which lamp heated the fastest? the slowest? Explain.

According to the graphs made in FIGS. 22-8 through 22-12, the green light gave the highest slopes of temperatures recorded. The red lamp was the coolest. Shouldn't the blue light have been the hottest? Explain.

QUESTIONS

In the late 1890s, American astronomer Annie Jump Cannon worked out a spectral classification for stars:

O B A F G K M R N S

Type O, R, N, and S stars are very rare. The O star class is quite hot (more than 30,000 degrees Celsius); the M star class is quite cool (less than 3,000 degrees Celsius). There are 10 subdivisions within each class. They range from 0 to 9. Thus, every star can be categorized.

To which spectral class does our Sun belong? What type of star will it evolve into in 5 billion years?

What spectral class does the star nearest us (Alpha Centauri) belong to? Could this sun be a part of a planetary system?

EARTH EVENT

Perform this experiment again, but use a white lamp for the heating/cooling. How do the temperatures recorded compare to the ones with the different colored lamps?

Test tube rack with
five test tubes

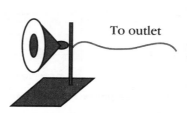

To outlet

Three equipment setups similar to this
are spread throughout the room.
The lights used are 100-watt: Red,
Green, and Blue.

22-1 Heating/cooling of actual land forms with a red, green, and blue sun

Heating time (minutes)	Substance temperature (°C)				
	Sand	Dirt	Grass	Salt water	Tap water
0					
1					
2					
3					
4					
5					
6					
7					
8					
9					
10					

22-2 Heating data table (red lamp)   Red

Heating time (minutes)	Substance temperature (°C)				
	Sand	Dirt	Grass	Salt water	Tap water
0					
1					
2					
3					
4					
5					
6					
7					
8					
9					
10					

Green

22-3   Heating data table (green lamp)

Heating time (minutes)	Substance temperature (°C)				
	Sand	Dirt	Grass	Salt water	Tap water
0					
1					
2					
3					
4					
5					
6					
7					
8					
9					
10					

Blue

22-4   Heating data table (blue lamp)

Cooling time (minutes)	Substance temperature (°C)				
	Sand	Dirt	Grass	Salt water	Tap water
11					
12					
13					
14					
15					
16					
17					
18					
19					
20					

22-5   Cooling data table (red lamp)   Red

Cooling time (minutes)	Substance temperature (°C)				
	Sand	Dirt	Grass	Salt water	Tap water
11					
12					
13					
14					
15					
16					
17					
18					
19					
20					

22-6   Cooling data table (green lamp)   Green

Cooling time (minutes)	Substance temperature (°C)				
	Sand	Dirt	Grass	Salt water	Tap water
11					
12					
13					
14					
15					
16					
17					
18					
19					
20					

Blue

22-7 Cooling data table (blue lamp)

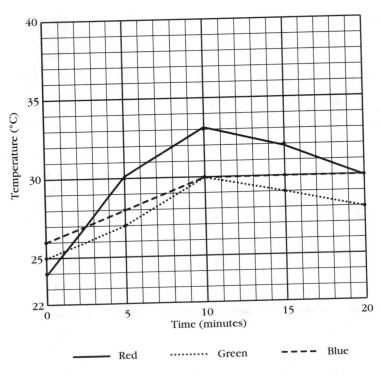

22-8 Sample graph (sand)

22-9 Sample graph (dirt)

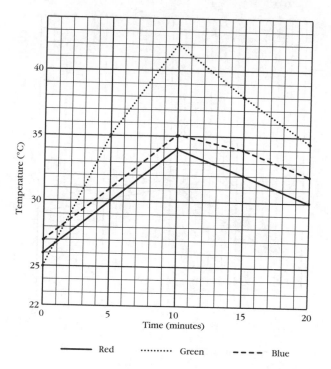

22-10 Sample graph (grass)

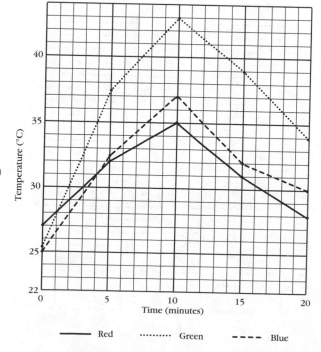

Heating/cooling of actual land forms with a red, green, & blue sun **105**

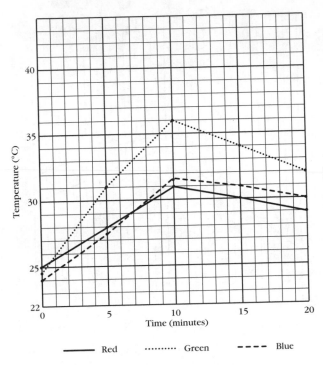

22-11 Sample graph (salt water)

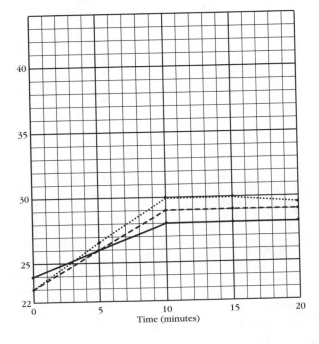

22-12 Sample graph (tap water)

☆ ☆ FACTOIDS ☆ ☆

The following facts have been paraphrased from a variety of sources (nearly 400): TV, magazines, research papers, newspapers, and reference books:

- Two conditions are needed for a "dust devil" (a whirlwind caused by rising warm air). The first is a hot surface such as a desert floor or freshly plowed field. Such a surface produces an updraft between 5 to 10 miles per hour. The second is a gentle horizontal breeze that blows from 2 to 5 miles per hour.

- A parcel of air that has traveled to California over 3,000 miles of Pacific ocean has nearly unlimited visibility. By the time it reaches the Midwest, this same parcel has a visibility from 10 to 15 miles. At the East Coast, this parcel has less than 7 miles visibility. The reason? A great deal of pollution and dust are picked up along the way by prevailing winds.

- Cosmic dust particles are so small, less than 0.01 microns (a micron is one millionth of a meter), that these particles can drift into the Earth's atmosphere and settle on the planet without melting on the way down.

- Even though the planet Saturn has a mass 95 times greater than Earth's, if an ocean existed that could hold Saturn, Saturn would float. Saturn is much less dense than water (water has a density of 1.00 g/ml).

- Of all the planets in our Solar System, Jupiter spins the fastest. Its day is slightly less than 10 hours (compared to Earth's 24-hour day.) If you could stand at the equator at Jupiter, your rotational speed would be 45,000 kilometers per hour! Compare this to the Earth's equatorial speed of 1,600 kilometers per hour. The length of daylight on Jupiter is only about 5 hours.

- On any given day, more than one thousand tons of micrometeorites fall to the Earth. In fact, you probably walked on some on your way to school.

- If the Moon's diameter was less than 2,000 miles (instead of 2,160 miles), or farther away so that it appeared smaller, people on Earth would never see an eclipse of the sun.

Heating/cooling of actual land forms with a red, green, & blue sun   107

Appendix A

Other fun phenomena

Here are twenty-five simple experiments for any grade level. Most are only 5 to 15 minutes in length if used as a demonstration in the classroom. Some require the growth of certain plants before beginning the experiment. All should be "fun" and quite understandable.

These should be springboards to explore certain concepts further. With adequate materials (borrowed from the school lab), they can also be performed at home under adult supervision. Wear goggles when using any open flames.

1. LIGHT SPECTRUM

Watch a surface of liquid crystal change in color indicating different temperatures. Obtain a liquid crystal cardboard square—6 inches by 6 inches. (Available from an equipment supply outlet; see the list of equipment manufacturers at the end of this book.)

Shine different colored lamps (of low wattage—25 watts is recommended) at this square. Watch how the liquid crystal square slowly changes color from a light brown or green to a deep blue color. (Brown or green colors indicate cooler temperatures; a dark blue color represents a higher temperature.)

2. HEAT FROM FRICTION

Shake an Erlenmeyer flask (250 ml), partially filled with sand. Use a one-hole rubber stopper and an alcohol thermometer pushed through to measure sand temperature. Measure the temperature of the sand before shaking the flask. Shake vigorously for at least a minute. Check the temperature again.

How much has it changed?

3. NAPKIN BALLOON

Observe the lifting influence of a convection cycle using a simple folded paper napkin. Fold the napkin at its corners, forming a rectangular (pan-like) shape.

Under adult supervision, drop this "parachute" from a two-story building on a hot day. A hot day will produce more unusual rising air currents. Compare this parachute with a crumpled napkin dropped at the same time. How effective is the shape of this model in floating?

4. ICE WATER BELOW 0° CELSIUS

Fill two 500-ml glass beakers with 250 ml of tap water. Next, fill both beakers with equal amounts of crushed ice. Place an alcohol thermometer into each mixture. Stir.

Read the temperatures on each thermometer. Now, pour at least 100 grams of table salt into one of the beakers. Stir thoroughly. What temperature does the thermometer indicate after stirring? Why is this? Why is salt sprinkled on a roadway after a winter snow/ice storm?

5. CLOUD IN A BOTTLE

You will need a large *glass* (not plastic) 5 gallon water bottle; a plastic bottle will not produce the cloud effect since its walls are flexible and move.

Obtain a bicycle tire pump and about 6 feet of rubber tubing (used to supply bunsen burners with the methane gas). Plastic aquarium tubing should not be used as it is not flexible enough and could kink, blocking flow of air into the bottle.

Use a solid rubber stopper that will form a very tight seal on the glass water jug. Drill a hole into this stopper. The diameter should be substantially less than the rubber tubing outer diameter. This will ensure a snug fit for the tubing.

Next, push the rubber tubing through this hole. A ballpoint pen works well in cramming this tubing into the hole. Push at least 6 inches through the hole.

Test the air pump by pumping several times. Air should be felt pushing out of the end of the rubber tubing.

Now, pour at least 10 ml of water into the glass jug. Light a match and drop it into the jar. Let it go out. When smoke is seen wisping up from the burnt match, dip the rubber stopper in a container of water.

Push the stopper onto the jug firmly. Since it is moistened, it will provide a nice seal.

Pump air into the glass jar. About 20 to 30 pumps depending on the size of the tire pump.

Stop pumping and then remove the rubber stopper from the jug. Watch what occurs. Why does this cloud float? How is this similar to opening a chilled soda can?

6. ALCOHOL AND WATER "THERMOMETERS"

Fill two 250-ml Erlenmeyer flasks with 150 ml each: distilled water in the first, and isopropyl alcohol in the second. Put several drops of food coloring (different colors) in each one. Stir.

With a one-hole rubber stopper and a piece of glass tubing—at least 50 cm in length (fire polished at both ends—see "Experiment preparation techniques" on page xxi), twist the rubber stopper onto the glass tubing. Use soapy water!

Now, carefully push the rubber stopper/glass tubing onto the flask. Push the stoppers into the flasks until each column begins to rise due to the pressure. The column should travel at least halfway up the glass.

Now, carefully push the rubber stopper tightly onto the flask. Be sure the two columns are at equal heights. If one is less than the other, take the stopper out and repeat the above procedure.

The thermometers are now ready. Hold one flask in each hand, letting the warmth of your hand push the different columns of liquid to different heights. The speeds of the rising and lowering liquids will be different also. Place these flasks in hot water and then ice water. Why would the water thermometer be inaccurate to use at temperatures below 0° Celsius?

7. SOAP BUBBLE FILM

Bombard it with different colored light to observe the colors reflected from its thin film. Create this soap film using a dish washing detergent (liquid preferred). Mix it with water and some glycerin in the following ratios: soap to water to glycerin (2 to 8 to 1).

Use low-wattage lamps (25) of the following colors: red, green, blue, and amber. Shine these lamps (either one at a time or several at once) at the soap films. What different colors show when different lamps are used? How are they different than when the white lamp is used?

8. SOLARIZING SOIL

This method used in gardening replaces chemical fumigation of the soil. A small model can be built for the classroom. Use a flat plastic pan at least 13 inches wide. Place soil in it to a depth of least 3 inches. Mix at least two handfuls of mulch into the soil.

Water this soil/mulch combination thoroughly and deeply. Place two thermometers in the soil (one at the surface, the other approximately 1 inch into the soil). Cover the entire pan with clear, heavy duty plastic. Seal this plastic covering tightly around the pan's edges with duct tape.

Place the entire unit outside in direct sunlight. (To compare the heating temperatures, fill an identical pan with soil, mulch, and water, but do not cover.)

Over a period of several days, observe the temperatures of the surface as well as the below the surface of each pan. How do they compare? Could such high temperatures be effective enough to sterilize the covered soil?

Try planting in the soil in both pans after several weeks. (After the cover is removed, let the soil cool for a day.) On the uncovered pan, pour water in the soil to soften the mixture for planting. Use radish or rye grass seeds. They grow quite quickly.

How is this procedure used in the covered pan related to a greenhouse effect?

9. CASTING A FLAT EARTH'S SHADOW ON A MODEL MOON

Cut a large circular disk out of wood. (About 15 inches in diameter by ¾ inch thick is an excellent size.)

If this is performed outside, make sure it is a sunny day. Cast the shadow from this disk onto a wall or the ground. (The wall or the ground is the model moon's surface.) Turn the disk as if to simulate the rotating Earth. Watch how a circular shape becomes a straight line. Note: Do not rotate the disk about its center, instead turn the disk as if there is an axis (or diameter) piercing this disk at its "edge."

In a darkened room, cast a shadow from this disk onto a wall using a bright flashlight. Keep the disk about 3 feet from the wall. Now, turn the disk slowly as if simulating the rotation of this flat "Earth." Watch how a circle shadow cast on the wall becomes a straight line.

In a sense, this is exactly the shadow that would be projected onto the moon during the many phases it undergoes due to Earth's blocking of sunlight.

Does this conclusively prove the Earth is not flat? Sadly, it does not. There is a small group of people who maintain the Earth is flat. But everyone is entitled to their beliefs of one form or another.

10. ATTEMPTING COMBUSTION IN A CARBON DIOXIDE ATMOSPHERE

Tape with masking tape four or five wooden "strike anywhere" matches to the inside bottom of a clean and dry, clear glass mayonnaise jar.

Next, place a tea candle in a pan of water approximately ¼ inch deep. Don't drown the candle. Be sure the pan is wide enough to hold the bottom of the jar.

Light the candle. Turn the jar upside down over the candle. Hold the top of the jar as it is inverted. What will happen to the candle flame?

After the candle is extinguished (the jar should stay inverted easily on its own), obtain a magnifying glass.

Take the pan/jar combination and (be careful not to lose the "seal" the jar opening has made with the water), carefully carry it outside on a sunny day (late morning or early afternoon nearly-direct sun rays are best). Set the jar down on a bench away from any dry brush or trees.

Attempt to light the matches inside the jar with the magnifying glass. Will they light? Why or why not? What gases are inside the jar? See if you can "flare up" all the matches inside the jar.

According to Hazardous Materials Specialist Steve Baker (no relation) of the Fire Protection District, County of Ventura, California:

A "fire triangle" is made of three items: a heat source, fuel, and a source of oxygen. It is quite possible Baker said that oxygen is still present in the inverted glass jar, but in an amount much too small to sustain either life or continued combustion.

11. LIGHT SPECTRUM (II)

Using a cardboard square with liquid crystal in it (obtainable from one of the Equipment Manufacturers at the end of this book), shine the spectrum of the sun onto it using a glass prism. Which color is the coolest? warmest?

12. TRANSPIRATION OF PLANTS

Obtain a potted plant with large green leaves. Wrap a plastic bag around it tightly. The following day, observe any changes inside the bag.

13. TRANSPIRATION OF PLANTS

Observe a mass change this time. Use two of the same plants. Bag one completely as in the above exercise. Hang both with strong string from a wooden plank (several meter sticks taped together) at opposite ends.

Tie a strong string to the middle of the plank. The two plants should balance each other and the plank should be level with the ground. Hang the assembly in a part of the room where it will not be disturbed by anyone.

The next day, observe the positions of the plants. Are they both level? What happened to the moisture in both plants?

14. FREEZE A SOAP BUBBLE

You'll need a glass aquarium, several large pieces of "dry ice" (frozen carbon dioxide), and soap bubble solution. Use *heavy duty* gloves to handle the dry ice. Place the pieces throughout the bottom of the tank. Wait several minutes for carbon dioxide gas to cover the bottom.

Blow several bubbles into the tank. The bubbles will float for several moments above the dry ice. Some will stick to the sides of the tank. Others will stick to the ice itself without popping. Watch these carefully.

Soon, the whole bubble will crystallize and become a solid, fragile shell of a frozen hollow sphere.

Poke the exterior with a glass stirring rod (not your finger!) and watch the bubble break into several frozen pieces.

15. MINIATURE OCEAN ECOSPHERE

Obtain a canning glass "jelly" jar with lid and liner. Be sure the inner cap is new and has a new rubber seal. A 16-oz (500-ml) jar works best. Fill this jar with actual ocean water nearly ¾ full.

Twist the lid on tightly and place the jar in indirect sunlight. If you have more than one jar, place several inside and outside the classroom. Over a period of several weeks, is anything forming in or on the water in the jar?

16. MINIATURE POND (OR GUTTER WATER) ECOSPHERE

Instead of sea water, use pond water or water (that has been standing) in a gutter. Seal the jar tightly. Watch the container for two or more weeks. Is there anything forming on or in the water? Why or why not?

17. CONVECTION CYCLE WITH ICE AND WATER

Using a 500 ml beaker (or very large glass jar), fill three-fourths with very hot water from the tap. Drop one ice cube in the container. Place several drops of food coloring immediately in after the ice drops into the jar or beaker. Watch what happens. What direction is the convection cycle moving in the beaker?

18. WATER BOILING IN A PAPER CUP

Fill a paper cup approximately half full with tap water. Using protective gloves, hold the cup directly over a bunsen burner flame until the water inside starts to bubble and boil. Why doesn't the cup burn?

19. WATER AS A POOR THERMAL CONDUCTOR

Fill a test tube with tap water. Tie a small metal weight to a small piece of ice. Drop this ice into the test tube. The ice should rest at the bottom of the tube.

Place the test tube in a burner flame. Tilt the tube so only the top portion of the water in the test tube is heated. As the water bubbles and starts to boil at the top, the ice at the bottom of the test tube does not melt.

20. THE MELTING POINT OF ICE IS RAISED BY PRESSURE

Tie two weights (at least 500 g) to each end of a piece of solid bare copper wire between the sizes number 16 to number 20.

Drape the wire over a large piece of block ice. Allow the ends of the wire to hang freely. As gravity tugs at the weights, watch the path the wire on top of the ice makes.

As the wire cuts through the ice, it melts the ice below. However, above the wire, the ice will refreeze. If left alone, the wire will cut completely through the block and the ice will remain whole.

This is similar in principle to a performing ice skater. The sharp metal blade is pushing quite hard on the ice. It briefly turns the ice below the blade into water. Technically, the person is skating on water.

21. DRY SAND VS. WET SAND: WHICH RETAINS HEAT BETTER?

Fill two 500-ml beakers each with 300 ml of dry sand. Place an alcohol thermometer into each. Pour 100 ml of water into one beaker, soaking the sand thoroughly.

Wait 5 minutes. Record the temperature of the sand in each beaker. Place both beakers into a refrigerator. Wait at least 20 minutes. What are the sand temperatures now? How did the water in the sand affect its temperature? Does it act as an insulator?

22. DRY SAND VS. WET SAND: WHICH HEATS FASTER?

Use the equipment as you did in Problem 21. After the beakers are taken out of the refrigerator, record their temperatures.

Place both beakers in noon-day sunlight (or under a 100-watt lamp) for at least 15 minutes. What are the sand temperatures after heating? How did the water affect the sand temperatures? How does living near the coast prevent temperature extremes for the residents?

23. SUNLIGHT ABSORPTION OF DIFFERENT COLORED PIECES OF DRY CLOTH

Use at least 8 to 10 "snippets" (3 by 3 cm squares) of different-colored fabric of the same type. (Pieces of excess fabric are available at any fabric store for the asking.)

Wrap each piece around an alcohol thermometer's bulb. Tape them tightly to the thermometer. Place the thermometers in direct sunlight or under a 100-watt white lamp.

Which covered thermometer has the lowest temperature reading? the highest? Explain how the different-colored clothing you wear on a summer or winter day is affected by the outside temperatures.

24. EVAPORATION OF WATER VAPOR FROM DIFFERENT-COLORED CLOTHING

Use the equipment you used in Problem 23. Be sure the thermometer temperatures are at room temperature. Dip each thermometer into a beaker of room temperature tap water. Place them outside in direct sunlight or under a 100-watt white lamp. If the lamp is used, direct the breeze of a fan at the thermometers.

How quickly did the fabric dry? Which thermometer had the lowest reading? Which changed the most rapidly? Why would hanging clothes out to dry on a sunny, windy day dry them more quickly than a cool, cloudy day?

25. THERMAL RADIATION TRAVELS IN STRAIGHT LINES

When a total solar eclipse occurs, the portion of the Earth in the darkest part of the shadow (umbra), cools quite significantly.

Using a 100-watt white lamp with a metal lamp shield, cast the light onto a wall from three feet away. Tape a thermometer to the wall where the light is strongest. The readings should climb significantly over the course of 5 to 10 minutes.

Place a sphere of suitable size (soccer or basket ball) on a table about a foot from the wall. Using another thermometer at room temperature (or wait until the first cools) tape it to the wall.

Cast the lamp's light onto the ball. Point out the umbra (dark shadow) and the penumbra (light shadow) that is cast onto the wall from the ball. Is the reading on the thermometer affected while in the darkest shadow of the sphere? Which shadow portion is the coolest? Explain.

Appendix **B**

Earth...& beyond

These questions require the use of only one tool to answer them . . . your mind. They will take you to distant worlds revolving about distant suns. There is much to imagine the existence of: life (sentient or otherwise), the lands, oceans, and the skies that make up the atmospheres.

I find it comforting to know that somewhere, perhaps only twenty light years away, that possibly a radio message is being transmitted to us after others received our commercial TV megawatt transmissions of the 1960s. Will we receive a message by the turn of the century? It is a lovely hypothesis. To discover that we are not alone would immediately make us all citizens of the Earth, a human unity.

These are also discussion questions. It is quite possible that a simple experiment could be developed to test a portion of one of these.

Essays of a fiction/non-fiction approach can be written for each question if desired.

These could also be potential science fair questions. All that is needed is imagination and a great deal of visualizing the extraordinary. Perhaps one day humans will venture to such distant worlds. One day some of these questions will be answered, but many more will then be raised.

Enjoy your travels.

1. On a planet with rocky features that appear slanted in the same direction, what possible weathering could account for such shaping?

2. Where might fossils of ancient life on the Moon be found? Why wouldn't they be found on the surface?

3. How is it possible for the planet Mercury to have ice caps at its poles even though that planet is so close to the sun?

4. Is it possible life on our planet emerged from cometary matter crashing into our atmosphere at the right moment when the building blocks of life were being formed in a lightning-filled atmosphere?

5. How did the Mount Tambora volcano (Tambora Sumbawa, Indonesia) explosion of April 5-7, 1815, change the weather patterns several years after its occurrence? (More than 100 cubic kilometers of dust was ejected, compared to the 1 cubic kilometer ejected by Mount St. Helens in Washington State.)

6. On a planet with two or more suns, what would the shape of rainbows take? Is there a simple experiment that could model this possibility?

7. How might plant life adapt to the different-colored light from two suns? Would its "photosynthesis" capability be limited only to these two colors?

8. Coleus Blumei, a multi-colored leafy plant, grows quite easily and makes easily grown cuttings. What would happen to the coloring of the leaves if it were grown under a red light or in a "sky" of a green-colored plastic shade? Can an experiment be designed to test this?

9. How does a magnetic field affect the growth of plant life? On other planets, how might such a field (stronger than Earth's) affect vegetation growth?

10. On a planet with two or more suns, assuming life exists and has adapted to this much sunlight, what would happen if one (or more) of the suns went nova? How much of the existing life would adapt to this sudden lack of light? Would it be likely that any of the existing life could adapt and survive?

11. What sort of studies of mythology and astronomy would be undertaken by intelligent aliens on a planet who see (instead of a moonrise) an entire spinning galaxy rising over their horizon at dusk or "sunrise?"

12. On a planet with multiple suns, how would a "sundial" or other timekeeping device using shadow lengths be built and calibrated?

13. Would the erosional capability of water (from any flowing rivers or streams) be any different on a planet if the planet's gravity were more or less than that of Earth's? (On Earth, 1 g = 9.8 m/sec/sec or 32 ft/sec/sec.)

14. From Question 13, would erosion of this same planet be more or less pronounced than that occurring on Earth if any "rain" falling were twice or one-half the density of water?

15. What sort of recreation for inhabiting "health-conscious" aliens would they engage in on a planet with a gravitational pull one-half or twice that of Earth's? How well would such a being perform some of our Olympic events here on Earth?

16. How does a different-colored light affect the spinning rate of a radiometer? (Use a 100-watt red, green or blue lamp to simulate a sun.) Be sure to have the lamps at least 25 cm away from the radiometer.

17. Will a radiometer (used in the above question) spin if a fluorescent lamp (a long mercury vapor lamp) is used? Why or why not?

18. Again reusing the radiometer, how will it spin if the spectrum of the sun is shone at it? Use a glass prism to cast the colors onto the radiometer leaves within its bulb.

19. Certain species of cactus turn their "leaves" to or away from the sun's rays depending on the time of day. Early or late in the day, it faces the sun to receive maximum solar radiation. When the sun is in the late morning or early afternoon elevation, the cactus orients itself to present as little of itself to the sun to prevent any extra evaporation. How would such a desert plant grow on a planet with two or more suns?

20. How would rainfall be distributed on a planet with more or less ocean-to-land ratio (surface areas only) than the Earth's (70 to 30?) (Hint: Use the simple classification of climate into tropical, temperate, and polar zones at the designated latitudes; 90° N, 60° N, 30° N, equator, 30° S, 60° S, and 90° S.)

21. How would the weather patterns be different if the Earth rotated instead of from West to East, but East to West?

22. What makes a cloud float above the Earth?

23. On planets with greater gravitational pull than Earth's (2, 3 or 4 times the acceleration of gravity) why would a cloud continue to float in the sky? Hint: Think of the cloudy gaseous ball of Jupiter.

24. Planets that are continually cloudy (Venus, for example), receive less energy at their surfaces than planets that generally are clear. Why, then, is Venus so hot at its surface?

25. How would extremely tall mountains (such as Mt. Olympus on Mars) affect rainfall on this planet by orographic uplift (mountain-modified winds)?

26. High speed winds of at least 200 miles per hour exist on Venus. Assume, for a moment, that a liquid ocean exists as well. What patterns in the ocean currents would such high speed winds form? (Hint: In 1855, an American naval officer named Matthew Maury compiled and published a book of how winds affected currents in the Atlantic Ocean. This had extensive data gathered by him.)

27. Ocean currents, like wind, are influenced by the Coriolis Effect (by Earth's rotation). On a non-rotating planet (such as Venus, where its length of day nearly equals its length of year) would there be any deflection of such wind or ocean currents?

28. How do oceans on Earth control the amount of carbon dioxide gas in the atmosphere? (Hint: This gas can dissolve in water. Think of a carbonated soft drink, for example.) Can a simple model be constructed that can help answer this question?

29. How would an artesian well work on a planet with a different gravitational acceleration than Earth's? (Earth is 9.8 meters/sec/sec or 32 feet/sec/sec.)

30. Would more water evaporate from ocean water in a pan of hot or cold water? Can an experiment be developed to test this?

31. Suppose humans find a way to destroy large hurricanes as soon as they appear. Would this be detrimental to the general circulation patterns on the Earth? Or, would the prevention of damage and saving of any lives counteract such negative effects from this manipulation?

32. How would the average temperature at the surface of Earth be affected if the amount of water vapor were greatly increased in its atmosphere?

33. If all the material in the sun could be sufficiently cooled to make the sun a solid body, what would be its mass?

34. Describe how the present atmospheres to the following planets developed: Venus, Earth, Mars, Jupiter, and Saturn. How are these atmospheres related to each other? Does each planet have an atmosphere of layers significantly different from one another?

35. How would the weather patterns on Earth be changed if the axis of rotation (through both North and South Poles) was suddenly changed to be the equator? In other words, the Earth is now spinning on its "side." Are there any planets in our solar system that have the axis located like this?

36. If the gravitational pull were twice that of Earth's (approximately 10 meters/sec/sec) what would the erosional patterns possibly be from a typical rainfall over land? over desert?

37. Continuing with Question 36, describe the damage to plants, vegetation, or

animals if a hailstorm occurred on a planet with twice Earth gravity.

38. Would there be any seasons on Earth if it had no 23.5° tilt? Explain.

39. How might the bone structure (the supportive skeletal system) of sentient beings or animals be different on a planet with twice or three times the gravitational pull of Earth's? If such a being visited Earth, would it be easier to move around? Or would it lead to clumsiness (and possible injury) to such a life-form?

40. What is the source of energy that makes the hydrologic cycle function on Earth?

41. On planets farther from the Sun than Earth, how does the erosion of that planet's landscape compare to ours? (Hint: On Earth, solar energy evaporates any surface water, which will fall to the ground again as rain or snow. The water will erode any land forms in its path. Wind and waves also derive their energy from the sun. A planet farther away than Earth will receive less solar energy.)

42. Gravity causes a downward motion of rock and soil debris. This is known as "mass-wasting." On Earth, such deposits move downhill in a process called creep. How might the rate of creep vary on a planet with a larger or smaller gravitational pull than the Earth's?

43. Some river or stream patterns on Earth consist of branch-like growths (dendritic), much like the branches on an oak tree. How does gravity play a part in such a stream movement or shape? Would a higher gravitational pull (on another planet) make larger or deeper stream branches?

44. Why is the sky clear over the eye of a hurricane? (Hint: Air is compressed as it flows downward and warmed, which decreases its relative humidity.)

45. In what part of the atmosphere do jet streams occur? What is their general direction of flow?

46. Describe a katabatic wind. Might such a wind exist on the planet Mars?

47. Why can't there exist a doldrums region on Venus or Mercury?

48. As air rises from the surface of the Earth, it cools at a certain rate called the lapse rate. For dry air, it is 5.5° Fahrenheit every 1000 feet. It is an adiabatic process. (No heat is exchanged between the air and its surroundings.) Would a parcel of carbon dioxide rising from the surface of Mars cool at a different rate? Why or why not?

49. Describe the layers of the atmosphere that exist on other planets: Mercury, Venus, Mars, Jupiter, Saturn, Uranus, and Neptune. How different are these atmospheres from Earth's? Are the layers more pronounced, or does the entire atmosphere blend into the planet itself like a bottomless pit?

50. How might insolation (incoming solar radiation) be different on the above-mentioned planets? (Hint: Solar radiation is scattered on its way to Earth by air molecules and dust, absorbed/reflected by atmospheric gases and dust, reflected/absorbed by clouds and reflected/absorbed by land forms.)

51. Why are clear nights more likely to be colder than cloudy nights?

52. How will the Great Flood of 1993 benefit the agriculture and farms in the Midwest for the next 10 to 20 years?

53. If oxygen and nitrogen gases in our atmosphere were not replaced, how long would the present supply last?

54. How is the size of a continent (here on Earth) related to monsoon size and occurrence?

Appendix **C**

Equipment manufacturers

Contact the following companies for catalogs or other information. Often, a high school or college science department will lend certain equipment or chemicals to use at your school.

A & A ENGINEERING
2521 W. La Palma Ave.
Anaheim, CA 92801
(714) 952-2114
Electronic equipment: power supplies, satellite receivers, and decoders.

CAROLINA BIOLOGICAL SUPPLY CO.
2700 York Rd.
Burlington, NC 27215
(800) 547-1733

EDMUND SCIENTIFIC CO.
101 E. Glouchester Pike
Barrington, NJ 08007-1380
Ordering Number: (609) 573-6250
Product Information: (609) 573-6259

FISHER SCIENTIFIC
4901 W. LeMoyne St.
Chicago, IL 60651
(800) 621-4769

FREY SCIENTIFIC CO.
905 Hickory La.
Mansfield, OH 44905
(800) 225-FREY

RADIO SHACK
(Check local listings in white pages of your telephone directory or call information.)
Electronic equipment: VHF weather radios.

SARGENT-WELCH SCIENTIFIC CO.
7300 North Linder Ave.
PO Box 1026
Skokie, IL 60077
(312) 677-0600

SCIENCE KIT & BOREAL LABORATORIES
777 East Park Dr.
Tonawanda, NY 14150-6782
(800) 828-7777

Appendix **D**

Answers to lab questions

The following answers were obtained at Thousand Oaks High School, in Southern California during the summer months: June, July, and August.

Every experiment has been done at least twice. Several were done three or four times.

Hence, while it could be said that these particular answers are "on target," their validity could only extend to my location with temperature, pressure and humidity peculiar to it.

Keep this in mind. Your results are just as valid. Remember, the goal of this science book (or any science text) is to perform as a tool. Such use can only sharpen its focus for future investigations.

All results in the laboratory room occurred at approximately 21° Celsius (room temperature). The outdoor experiments were performed on sunny, cloudless days.

It must be noted here that the month of July 1993 saw very few sunny mornings. This is quite extraordinary for Southern California weather.

EXPERIMENT 1
Observations

See your data and graph.
See your data and graph.

Questions

The blue lamp should heat more intensely.
The temperatures should plateau, but your data times will be different.

EXPERIMENT 2
Observations

See your data table.
The salt water most likely heated faster. The impurities (sodium chloride) absorb sunlight instead of permitting the light to pass through. This causes the water to heat faster than tap water.

Questions

Infrared radiation (IR) has a longer wavelength and hence a lower frequency of transmission. Ultraviolet radiation (UV) has a shorter wavelength and a higher frequency of transmission. Both portions are somewhat screened by the Earth's atmosphere.

The ozone layer absorbs most of the UV radiation striking the atmosphere of Earth.

Through the use (or misuse) of aerosols and refrigerants. There is a large hole over the South Pole. One is also forming over the North Pole as well.

EXPERIMENT 3

Observations

See your data table. Most likely the grass blades lost the most moisture. Fresh grass blades contain a great deal of water.

They were yellow, thin, and curled.

This could vary, but most likely the dirt lost more moisture.

The 2.0 ml of water was used to be a "baseline" for evaporation. If more than 2.0 ml of water was evaporated, then the inherent moisture in each sample was being evaporated. This lab was a test for the lamp to see how much of the initial water could be removed from each sample.

Questions

The desert area loses moisture (when it occurs from rain) at a very great rate. However, consistent water vapor loss occurs mostly at the equatorial regions in the ocean. This is where the sun's rays are the most direct.

EXPERIMENT 4

Observations

See your data table. Rock or sand color will affect heating rates.

See your data table.

The temperatures in the example data table did not plateau. Perhaps, if the experiment had been given more time to run, they would have leveled off.

Again, the cooler or warmer section varies with the rock/sand color.

Sunlight temperatures are roughly comparable to the white lamp temperatures.

Questions

The slope of a graph of material heating in a vacuum would be quite steep. The temperature would probably plateau higher. The atmosphere acts like an "insulating blanket." This prevents overheating or extensive heat loss to space.

EXPERIMENT 5

Observations

See your data table.

The motor warmed the air after it ran for several minutes. However, in an empty tank, no flying particles created any collisions. There was no extra friction, therefore no extra heating occurred. The only heating was found in the motor running.

The motor did contribute to the temperature increase, but in comparing both data tables (motor and motor/sand), there is more of an influence to heating done by the flying sand particles.

Questions

Carbon dioxide traps sunlight and this could contribute to the heating of Venus. Since one side faces the sun nearly all the time, excessive heating to the subsolar (sun-facing) side occurs.

EXPERIMENT 6

Observations

See your data table.

Compare the data to Experiment 7.

Questions

Probably the temperatures (of the completely blocked sun) would be as if there were one sun heating the surface.

More heating means more uplifted air. If air rises in one place (heated from the suns), it must sink in another (cooler air dropping down to the surface away from the suns). There would be more violent winds.

More moisture would be evaporated from the oceans. More carbon dioxide would be driven from surface rocks. This would contribute to more heating at the surface. The global temperatures would rise. This would then trigger more melting of the ice caps. More flooding would occur.

The position of the jet stream could shift more quickly during certain seasons of the year. This would cause more violent weather extremes.

EXPERIMENT 7

Observations

See your data table.

Compare these results to Experiment 6.

Questions

Probably the temperature heating effects would remain the same. As long as the luminosity and mass were kept the same, the results would be similar.

Winds would become more intense as the sun from "behind" emerges and contributes to the heating of the atmosphere.

EXPERIMENT 8

Observations

These were sources of temperature differentials. They aided in the start-up of the convection cycle by providing uneven temperatures.

Most likely, the orientation of the lamp will provide different heating cycles and patterns. In the "equatorial position," the lamp heated the base of the dirt mound.

See your data table.

It represents a simple model of a large convection cycle, but there are many other factors missing: forest biomes and rock/desert formations, are two such factors.

Questions

Heated parcels of gas on Venus would rise at the equator (subsolar point) and travel upward. They would migrate eventually over both poles to the "dark side" of Venus and sink at a point exactly opposite the subsolar point. This is known as the antisolar point. There would be two gigantic convection cycles: one over each pole.

EXPERIMENT 9

Observations

See your data table. The example data table used shows thermometers 4 and 2, 5, and 1 nearly equal in heating. The light heats the ground evenly all over, hence the temperatures will rise equally.

Thermometer 6 was influenced by the pan of water (it was closer than thermometer 3). Hence, it cooled more rapidly.

Questions

On a flat Earth, a ship would not "disappear" at all as it receded in the distance. Eventually, it would become a speck to the observer's eye on the horizon. The ship would then "fall off" the Earth when it reached the edge.

Eratosthenes was aware of a deep well in Syene that the Sun would exactly pass overhead and light the interior completely. When this happened, there was no shadow cast in Syene by objects. However, in Alexandria, at this same time, there were shadows cast by objects. Using just his brains, feet, and a desire to complete a mathematical problem, Eratosthenes calculated the circumference of the Earth with remarkable precision.

EXPERIMENT 10

Observations

The water prevented excessive temperature rises. Coastline dwellers have such a temperature regulator between water and land.

See your data table. Yes, darker sand or rock would heat differently than lighter sand or rock.

Questions

If an ocean of water could exist on the Moon, temperatures on both the sunny and dark side of the Moon would not be as extreme as compared to what the Moon's temperatures actually are now. Perhaps an atmosphere and ocean did exist one time when the Moon was volcanically active.

EXPERIMENT 11

Observations

Method I At both the 1 AU and 2 AU distances, the equator received the most direct light.

Both poles received indirect light, hence they did not heat as much as the other latitudes. See your data table for the answer to the second question.

Method II The "planet" at 1 AU received the most direct light. Its stabilized temperature was significantly higher than the temperatures at the other model planets.

At 5 AU, the observed temperature change would be quite small. At 10 AU, it would be difficult to measure it with an ordinary thermometer.

Questions

See your graph. Slopes for pole temperatures would be quite small. There would be very little rise to the lines.

EXPERIMENT 12

Observations

See your data table.

See your data table. The carbon dioxide atmosphere absorbed more heat and evaporated more water from the pan.

Questions

Mars has very little precipitable water in its atmosphere. If all the water vapor could condense on the planet's surface, it would amount to 0.001 inch. If all of Earth's water vapor condensed, it would cover the surface with 1 inch of water.

Most likely there would be more rainfall with more water vapor in the atmosphere. This would imply that greater temperatures globally had occurred (with the ice caps possibly melting). Is the Earth warming? Some experts think so. With such warming, wild storms and droughts would occur.

EXPERIMENT 13

Observations

See your data table. Heating temperatures depend on color of the substance.

See your data table. In the example data table, grass heated the highest amount. The moisture in the sealed test tube created a minor "greenhouse" effect.

See your data table. The salt water heated slightly faster than the tap water, according to the example data table results.

Questions

A different-colored sky could heat or cool the surface of the Earth much more differently than the existent blue sky.

Smoke from volcanic eruptions tends to act as an "insulating blanket," trapping heat. Thus, the surface below remains cooler.

Plant and animal life could very easily perish if the smoke layer cut off all light reaching the surface. A thinner cloud cover could let certain frequencies of light through. Some of the surface life (both plant and animal) could adapt and survive.

EXPERIMENT 14

Observations

Greatest to least evaporation: open-air aquarium, carbon dioxide atmosphere (sealed), air atmosphere (sealed).

Questions

Carbon dioxide absorbs more heat and causes more evaporation. The air atmosphere (sealed) did not absorb as much heat as the carbon dioxide. Therefore, the evaporation was not as great.

The open-air experiment is influenced by the classroom air currents and temperatures. A rainy day means the air is fairly humid. Evaporation would be less.

EXPERIMENT 15

Observations

See your data tables.

Carbon dioxide absorbs sunlight more than air. This causes more heating and cooling differences than air.

Questions

It causes Venus to have excessively high surface temperatures. Any sunlight is trapped and turned into heat.

Global temperatures will rise and it is possible that the ice caps could melt. This would trigger more flooding of coastlines.

EXPERIMENT 16

Observations

See your data tables.

The carbon dioxide absorbed more heat. This caused more evaporation. It is peculiar that with the example data table the most saline solution lost the most water. I do not know why this occurred.

Questions

The open aquarium was influenced by the classroom wind currents and temperatures. All samples of water (NaCl) evaporated equally (as seen in the example data tables).

EXPERIMENT 17

Observations

The apple half in open air (inside and outside the classroom) had the most oxidation.

The carbon dioxide tended to slow (or retard) oxidation effects. Oxygen (what little there was in the tank) could not readily strike the apple portion as quickly as it did in open air.

Questions

A piece of freshly cut fruit would shrink on the surface of Mars. The shrinkage would be due to the loss of water vapor. The apple half would become "mummified" as moisture is torn from the fruit. This atmosphere would certainly be an excellent freeze-drying oven. Most likely, the apple would oxidize little. Would it be edible? I do not know.

EXPERIMENT 18

Observations

The solution was stirred to distribute the cooling effects of the ice throughout the beaker.
See your data table.

Questions

The water ice would sink after freezing. The liquid above would stay as a liquid while the available amount of water moisture would enter the solid phase. This phase would correspond to the season during which this occurred. The surface liquid could possibly act as an "insulating blanket," perhaps partially melting the water ice. The water at the bottom would flow according to the pull of gravity.

EXPERIMENT 19

Observations

See your data table.

Since the 10.5% salt solution had more dissolved solids in it, this caused the ice molecules to collide with salt molecules and contribute to a more rapid melting. I do not know why distilled water would melt ice the quickest.

Questions

Icebergs in oceans of salinities greater than Earth oceans would melt faster than our icebergs.

More minerals are eroded from landscapes on planets with higher salinity oceans. These minerals contain much sodium chloride and other salts as well.

EXPERIMENT 20

Observations

Each light first casts a shadow opposite to the light. The object is directly in a straight line between both lamp and shadow. However, the anti-red and anti-blue shadows are "fill in" colors. The light from each lamp fills in the shadow directly in front of each lamp. This is known as the "Flammarion Effect."

The anti-red shadow was the coolest, according to the example data table. The anti-blue shadow was the warmest.

Since no light could reach behind the block (light travels in straight lines, as does thermal radiation), this area would be the darkest and coolest.

This was where the red and blue lights blended their respective anti-blue and anti-red shadows. A penumbra occurs when an object casts a shadow from sunlight onto the ground. If the object (such as a tree) has portions farther from the ground, light diffracts around the leaves and branches. Shadows of varying shades are produced.

Questions

These temperatures could be life sustaining to organisms sensitive to both light colors. An organism would have to be able to use both frequencies of light for photosynthesis to ensure survival when one sun is blocked by the other.

EXPERIMENT 21

Observations

See your data table.

The smoke layer inhibited any heating. It acted as an "insulating blanket."

Questions

Such a catastrophe like these would initially greatly affect the local weather. The sun would be "blotted out," possibly for days. This would cause much local cooling until atmospheric winds sifted the dust and smoke throughout the rest of the atmosphere.

A large volcanic eruption and a large meteorite crash could affect global weather. Mt. Tambora (April 1815) is an example of a volcano. The piece of comet or meteorite that struck the Tunguska Forest in Russia in 1908 is an example of outworldly influences on global weather.

EXPERIMENT 22

Observations

See your data tables.

It is possible that the green lamp contained a mixture of frequencies of light capable of heating more strongly than the blue lamp. One way to roughly verify this would be to view both colored lamps using a spectroscope. There would be more visible lines of the spectrum made by the green light as seen through the diffraction grating than from the blue light. However, blue light in general is warmer than green light; green light is warmer than red light.

Questions

Our sun is a type G-2 star. It will last for another 5 billion years. At some point after that, it will swell into a red giant. Mercury, Venus, and the Earth will be cooked by the expanding sun.

Alpha Centauri is a type G-2 star as well. Quite possibly there may be planets orbiting this star system.

Index

About the author

Thomas Baker is a full-time mathematics and science teacher at Westlake High School in Thousand Oaks, California. He holds two Professional Clear Teaching Credentials in mathematics, inclusive of calculus, and science (physics, chemistry, and earth science) from the California State University, Northridge. He is a member of and frequent presenter at the National Science Teachers Association conferences. He is also a member of the National Council for Teachers of Mathematics, the California Science Teachers Association, and the American Meteorological Society.

The author and his daughter Noel.